ANITA BEAN'S
SPORTS NUTRITION FOR WOMEN

ANITA BEAN'S
SPORTS NUTRITION
FOR WOMEN

Note
Whilst every effort has been made to ensure that the content of this book is as technically accurate and as sound as possible, neither the author nor the publishers can accept responsibility for any injury or loss sustained as a result of the use of this material.

Published in 2010 by A & C Black Publishers Ltd
36 Soho Square, London W1D 3QY
www.acblack.com

ISBN 978 14081 1407 0

A CIP catalogue record for this book is available from the British Library.

Acknowledgements
Cover photographs © Shutterstock (top) © BananaStock Ltd (bottom)
Inside photographs © Shutterstock 4, 11, 13, 15, 22, 26, 27, 29, 38, 40, 47, 55, 59, 64, 67, 69, 73, 78, 82, 86, 89, 92, 93, 95, 97, 99, 106, 113, 118, 122; © istockphoto.com 1
Illustrations by Jeff Edwards
Designed by James Watson
Commissioned by Charlotte Croft
Edited by Kate Turvey
This book is produced using paper that is made from wood grown in managed, sustainable forests. It is natural, renewable and recyclable. The logging and manufacturing processes conform to the environmental regulations of the country of origin.

Typeset in 11 on 12.5pt AGaramond by Palimpsest Book Production Limited, Grangemouth, Stirlingshire

Printed and bound in China by C&C Offset Printing Co

CONTENTS

INTRODUCTION

Why a book for female athletes? For the last 20 years or so I've been advising both male and female athletes on nutrition, and have realised that female athletes have different nutritional, weight and performance concerns compared with men. While men and women's basic nutritional needs may not be significantly different, female athletes often eat differently from male athletes in ways that may prevent them meeting their nutritional needs. Like women in general, female athletes are under social pressure to be thin, and this – combined with the physical and psychological demands of their sport – may lead to restrictive eating. Many attempt to achieve low body fat levels by unhealthy eating practices and compulsive exercise. While leanness is desirable for performance in many sports, it often comes at a price, and a large number of female athletes develop disordered eating and serious eating disorders such as anorexia nervosa.

Much research has focused on a condition known as the 'female athlete triad': disordered eating, amenorrhoea (the cessation of periods) and bone loss. These are often present simultaneously in female athletes who restrict their diets and under-nourish their bodies due to negative body image. Disordered eating is typically the trigger of the triad. Low calorie intakes combined with intense or excessive training can cause a woman's body fat level to fall so low that the ovaries can no longer produce enough oestrogen. This hormone is needed for normal menstrual function and bone formation, and low levels of it result in menstrual dysfunction (irregular or absent periods). This, combined with under-nutrition, results in a loss of bone density, and increased risk of stress fractures and osteoporosis.

Many athletes may not have the extreme symptoms of the triad, but rather may have 'sub-clinical' stages of one or more of the conditions. For example, an athlete may show signs of restrictive eating, but not meet the clinical criteria for an eating disorder. Or she may experience menstrual disturbances, such as a change in menstrual cycle length, but not yet have developed amenorrhea. Likewise, she may be losing bone, but may not yet have dropped below her age-matched normal range for bone density.

In writing this book, I wanted to provide female athletes with the very latest information about the female athlete triad, and help them to make decisions and find support. In addition, I think that it's important to recognise that female athletes come in all shapes and sizes, even within the same sport, and that very low body fat is not necessarily desirable – it may have a negative impact on a female athlete's health. Chapter 3 will help you understand the consequences of achieving an optimal weight and body composition for your sport, and enable you to put into practice a healthy weight loss strategy.

If you are pregnant, or considering having a baby in the future, then you will find plenty of practical information on conception, nutrition and exercise during pregnancy in Chapter 5. It addresses the unique nutritional concerns of female athletes, and presents the consensus of medical opinion on safe exercising during pregnancy.

To help you put the nutritional advice in this book into practice, I have devised more than 40 delicious recipes (starting on page 99) that are easy to prepare, and good for you too. Each provides a nutritional breakdown so you know exactly what you are eating!

I hope that you will find this book informative and helpful, and that it will inspire you to make positive changes to the way you eat and train.

Yours in health,
Anita Bean

01

THE NUTRITIONAL NEEDS OF FEMALE ATHLETES

Planning what you eat before, during and after exercise is important. A healthy diet will increase your energy and endurance, reduce fatigue and maximise your fitness gains. After exercise, you need to give your body enough of the nutrients it needs for repair and recovery.

To help you make the right food choices, this chapter explains the basis of a good training diet, what each nutrient does, how much you need and how you can achieve your ideal intake.

How does my body produce energy?

In your body, energy is produced from carbohydrate, fat, protein and alcohol. Carbohydrates are the body's preferred fuel, although protein, fat and alcohol can also be converted into energy. Each nutrient provides different amounts of energy. For example, 1 g of the nutrients listed below provides the amount of energy indicated:

- carbohydrate 4 kcal (17 kJ)
- fat 9 kcal (38 kJ)
- protein 4 kcal (17 kJ)
- alcohol 7 kcal (29 kJ).

Each body cell has a small store of readily available energy in the form of a compound called adenosine triphosphate (ATP): the energy 'currency' of your body. ATP consists of an adenosine 'backbone' with three phosphate groups attached. When one of these phosphate groups splits off, then energy is produced (see fig. 1.1). Around one-quarter of this energy fuels work (such as muscular movement); the rest is given off as heat. ATP is continually being made and broken down to keep up with your body's requirements for energy.

Normally, you have enough ATP in your muscle cells to fuel a few seconds of exercise; after this your body breaks down glucose (from your blood or from stored glycogen in your muscles) and/or fat to make more ATP and therefore more energy.

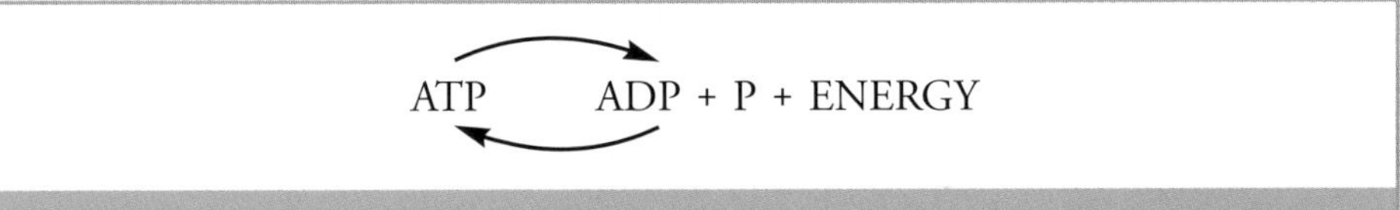

Fig 1.1 The relationship between ATP and ADP

You may be wondering if the source of the calories is important. If you are only considering weight loss or gain, the answer is no, it is the total intake of calories that is important. However, if you are talking about nutrition and health, it definitely does matter where your food calories come from. Generally, carbohydrates and proteins are healthier sources of calories than fats or alcohol.

What are calories?

Calories are the units used to describe the amount of energy in food. In scientific terms, one calorie is defined as the amount of energy (heat) required to increase the temperature of 1 gram of water by 1°C. A kilocalorie (kcal) is equal to 1000 calories.

What's the difference between calories, kilocalories and kilojoules?

You'll see all these terms on food labels, which can be a bit confusing! One kilocalorie (kcal) is 1000 calories, and this is strictly what we mean when speaking about 'calories' in the everyday sense. The scientifically defined calorie is a very small energy unit, which would be inconvenient to use on food labels. An average serving of any food typically provides thousands of these calories. For example, a food label would declare a portion of food contains 100 kcal rather than 100,000 calories. However, in everyday language we would probably say '100 calories'.

You'll also see food energy measured in joules or kilojoules (kJ) on food labels, which is the SI (standard international) unit for energy, named after Sir Prescott Joule. One joule is the energy required to exert a force of one Newton for a distance of one metre. Again, a joule is not a large amount of energy, so kilojoules (1 kJ = 1000 J) are more often used. One kcal is equivalent to 4.2 kJ.

How can I work out how many calories I need?

Your calorie needs depend on many factors: your genetic make-up, age, weight, body composition and your daily activity. They will differ from one day to the next, depending on your level of activity, and as you grow older if your lifestyle changes. The average (sedentary) woman needs around 2000 calories a day and men around 2500. These are the guideline daily amounts (GDAs) for energy that you see on food labels.

The number of calories you burn daily depends on three main factors:

1 your basal metabolic rate (BMR)
2 your level of physical activity
3 thermogenesis.

Your *BMR* is the number of calories you burn at rest to keep your heart beating, your lungs breathing, to maintain your body temperature, and so on. It accounts for 60–75 per cent of the calories you burn daily. Generally, women have a lower BMR than men, due to their smaller body mass.

The second factor, *physical activity*, includes all activities, from doing the housework to walking and working out in the gym. The number of calories you burn in any activity depends on your weight, the type of activity and the duration of that activity.

The third factor, *thermogenesis*, is the process by which the body generates heat by increasing the metabolic rate above normal. This occurs after consuming food, and includes the extra energy involved in eating, digesting and processing food – it's called the 'thermic effect of food'. Typically it accounts for about 10 per cent of your total calorie expenditure. So, if you eat 2000 calories a day, you'll burn about 200 calories digesting that food.

So, your daily calorie requirement is the sum of these three factors: BMR, physical activity and thermogenesis. It is possible to measure your daily calorie output (and therefore your calorie needs) by two methods: **indirect calorimetry** and the **doubly labelled water technique.** Both require specialised equipment and are generally limited to universities and research organisations.

With indirect calorimetry, the amount of oxygen you consume and carbon dioxide you produce is measured in a metabolic chamber (a sealed room unit) or in a 'ventilation hood', mask or mouthpiece, over several hours or days. The amount of energy you have expended is then calculated using various equations.

With the doubly labelled water technique, the concentration of non-radioactive isotopes in your urine is measured after ingesting a sample of water that has been labelled with non-radioactive isotopes of hydrogen and oxygen. This gives a measure of the amount of carbon dioxide, and therefore energy, produced by your body.

However, these methods are mostly used in the realms of research and are not very accessible to the general public. Instead, you can estimate your calorie needs and basal metabolic rate using predictive equations that take account of your weight and daily activity level. However, it is worth bearing in mind that these equations are based on populations of sedentary people, rather than athletes, so you should use them simply as a guide to your calorie needs.

Step 1: Estimate your basal metabolic rate (BMR) using either of the following methods.

Quick method

As a rule of thumb, BMR uses 22 calories for every 1 kg of a woman's body weight.

Women: BMR = weight in kg × 22

Example: BMR for a 60 kg woman = 60 × 22 = 1320 kcal.

Longer method

For a more accurate estimation of your BMR, use the Harris–Benedict equation:

BMR = 665 + (9.6 × W) + (1.8 × H) - (4.7 × age) = daily calorie needs
Where:
W = weight in kg
H = height in cm
Age = years

An example for a 30-year-old woman weighing 60 kg and measuring 168 cm (5 foot 6 inches) tall would be:

665 + (9.6 × 60) + (1.8 × 168) - (4.7 × 30)
665 + 576 + 302 - 141 = **1402** kcal per day

This equation will be accurate for most women except the extremely muscular (these women need more calories) and the extremely fat (these women need fewer calories), because it doesn't take into account the amount of lean body weight a person may have.

Step 2: Estimate your physical activity level (PAL)

Your physical activity level is the ratio of your overall daily energy expenditure to your BMR – a rough measure of your lifestyle activity.

Table 1.1 Working out PAL

Physical activity level (PAL)	Description	Examples
1	Inactive	Sleeping/lying down
1.2	Sedentary	Mainly sitting/desk job
1.5	Moderately active	Some walking
1.7	Active	Daily walking or gentle exercise
2.0	Very active	Moderate daily training or sport
2.2	Extremely active	Strenuous daily training or sport

Step 3: Multiply your BMR by your PAL

Daily calorie needs = BMR × PAL

So, the daily energy needs of a 30-year-old active 60 kg woman are:

1402 × 1.7 = 2383 kcal

This figure gives you an idea of your daily calorie requirement to maintain your weight. If you eat fewer calories, you will lose weight; if you eat more, you will gain weight.

Why do women need fewer calories than men?

Women generally have lower calorie requirements than men because they have less muscle tissue and, generally, weigh less. Muscle tissue burns more calories than fat. The more muscle mass you have, the more calories you will burn. And the heavier you are (whether that's muscle or fat), the higher your metabolic rate.

Do you need fewer calories as you get older?

As you get older, activity levels are often reduced, which causes a loss of muscle tissue, and so your energy requirements tend to decrease – but this isn't inevitable. Regular exercise (especially resistance training) can help reduce or prevent the 3.2 kg decline in muscle mass generally observed with each decade of ageing.

Is there a minimum calorie level I should have to stay healthy?

Severely restricting your calorie intake may lead to a drop in your performance as well as having serious health consequences. According to researchers at Ohio University in the USA, levels of female sex hormones fall and menstruation may become irregular or stop altogether (amenorrhoea – *see* Chapter 4). Studies with female athletes have shown that when calorie intake drops below a threshold of 30 kcal per kg of lean body weight per day, bone health is affected. There is increased bone loss, stress fractures and, in younger athletes, failure to achieve their peak bone mass.

It is thought that the combination of intense training, calorie restriction and the psychological pressure for extreme leanness may precipitate disordered eating and clinical eating disorders in some athletes. There is a fine line between dieting and obsessive eating behaviour, and many female athletes are under pressure to be thin and improve their performance. The warning signs and health consequences of eating disorders are discussed in Chapter 2.

Where do I get energy from during exercise?

Your muscles derive energy from carbohydrate, fat and protein during exercise, but the proportions of these fuels will depend on the type, intensity and duration of your activity, how well conditioned, or 'fit', you are, and what you have eaten beforehand.

During **anaerobic** activities, such as sprinting and weight lifting, virtually all the energy you burn comes from carbohydrates, or muscle glycogen (stored carbohydrate). On the other hand, during **aerobic** activities, such as running, swimming and cycling, energy is provided by a mixture of carbohydrates and fat. Protein may also fuel aerobic exercise – but its contribution becomes significant only when muscle glycogen stores become depleted.

The higher your exercise **intensity**, the greater the reliance on muscle glycogen. As a rule of thumb, during moderate exercise intensities (50–70 per cent of your maximal aerobic capacity) glycogen supplies around half your energy needs. At higher exercise intensities – above 70 per cent of your maximal aerobic capacity – it makes up around three-quarters of your energy supply.

The fuel mixture changes with exercise **duration**. As your muscle glycogen stores deplete, the muscles will use more fat, blood glucose and protein for energy. Generally, your muscles use a higher percentage of glycogen for fuel during the early stages of a workout, and a higher percentage of fat for fuel during the latter stages.

Aerobic conditioning (or 'fitness') affects the fuel mixture used during exercise. Regular aerobic training increases the levels of fat-burning enzymes in your muscle cells, which means your muscles learn to burn fat more readily and spare precious glycogen. This is clearly advantageous for endurance sports because the body's stores of fat energy are vastly greater than its store of glycogen energy (typically 400 g or 1600 kcal in a 70 kg person). In other words, the better conditioned you become, the more efficiently your muscles produce energy, and the longer you can continue exercising.

How much carbohydrate, fat and protein you burn during exercise also depends on your **pre-exercise diet**. Consuming carbohydrates during the two to four hours before exercise increases blood sugar and insulin levels, which encourages the muscles to favour carbohydrates for fuel. On the other hand, fasting or avoiding carbohydrates during the four-hour pre-exercise period encourages the muscles to burn a little more fat and less carbohydrate during exercise. The number of calories burned will not necessarily change, only the proportions of carbohydrate and fat.

What's the difference between liver and muscle glycogen?

The purpose of liver glycogen is to maintain steady blood sugar levels. When blood glucose dips, glycogen in the liver breaks down to release glucose into the bloodstream. Muscle glycogen, on the other hand, fuels physical activity. During exercise, glycogen in your muscles releases glucose, which is used for energy.

Eating and exercise: before, during and after

When and what should I eat before exercise?

Most of the energy needed for exercise is provided by whatever you have eaten several hours – indeed, days – before. A balanced diet that includes enough carbohydrate will produce high levels of glycogen in your muscles.

Ideally, you should have a light meal approximately two to four hours before exercising, according to researchers at the University of North Carolina. Leaving a longer interval between eating and exercising may reduce your endurance and result in earlier fatigue. They also recommend including moderately high amounts of carbohydrate and avoiding too much fat in your pre-exercise meal.

Opt for foods with a low glycaemic index (GI) – foods that produce a gradual rise in blood sugar levels. Researchers at the University of Sydney found that cyclists were able to exercise for 20 minutes longer after eating a low-GI meal (lentils) compared with a high-GI meal (potatoes). A 2006 study at the University of Loughborough found that runners who consumed a low-GI meal three hours before exercise were able to run on average eight minutes longer compared with those who

ate a high-GI pre-exercise meal. The slower release of energy helped maintain their blood sugar levels, reduced the rate at which muscle glycogen was burned and promoted fat burning. In other words, eating a low-GI meal will encourage your body to burn more fat and less glycogen during exercise, and will help to increase your endurance. Porridge, cereal with milk, a jacket potato with beans, or a light pasta dish would be suitable pre-workout meals.

If you plan to exercise for longer than one hour, having a low-GI pre-workout drink or snack 30–60 minutes before exercise may also benefit your performance. Try an apple, a few dried apricots, a handful of sultanas, a smoothie, a pot of yoghurt, 300 ml of diluted fruit juice (50/50) or even half a bar (25 g) of chocolate. The extra carbohydrates will help postpone fatigue.

PRE-EXERCISE SNACKS

- Fresh fruit
- Wholemeal toast with honey
- Cereal bar
- Fruit yoghurt
- Dried fruit
- Cereal with milk.

PRE-EXERCISE MEALS

Eat two to four hours before exercise.

- Sandwich/roll/bagel/wrap filled with chicken, fish, cheese, egg or peanut butter
- Jacket potato with beans, cheese, tuna, coleslaw or chicken
- Pasta with tomato-based pasta sauce, vegetables and cheese
- Macaroni cheese with salad
- Rice with chicken or fish, and vegetables
- Porridge made with milk
- Wholegrain cereal with milk or yoghurt.

What should I eat during exercise?

If you are exercising hard for more than 60 minutes, consuming an extra 30–60 g carbohydrate per hour may help delay fatigue and increase your endurance, according to studies at the University of Texas in the USA. During the latter stages of your workout, as glycogen stores dwindle, additional carbohydrate will help maintain blood glucose levels and thus provide additional fuel for your muscles. After 90–120 minutes of intense exercise, your muscles rely almost entirely on blood glucose and fat for fuel. Clearly, consuming extra carbohydrate would help you continue exercising longer.

Start refuelling after about 30 minutes – it takes around 30 minutes for the carbohydrates to get absorbed into your bloodstream – and then continue at regular intervals. Stick to 30–60 g per hour – any more can not be used by your muscles and therefore will not benefit your performance.

Choose high-GI carbohydrates, which convert into blood sugar rapidly. A drink containing between 1 and 6 g sugar per 100 ml (e.g. certain fruit drinks, sports drinks or diluted fruit juice) would provide the dual benefit of hydration as well as fuel. If you prefer consuming solid carbohydrate, such as cereal bars, energy gels, energy bars, bananas, fruit bars, low-fat biscuits (e.g. fig rolls), malt loaf, dried fruit or chocolate, you should also drink water to replace your fluid losses.

Studies at the University of Texas and James Madison University in Vancouver, Canada, have suggested that consuming a drink containing a little protein as well as carbohydrate (in a 1:4 ratio) during prolonged exercise may help increase endurance and speed recovery. Cyclists were able to continue exercising for 29 per cent longer when drinking carbohydrate with protein compared with carbohydrate alone. However, these drinks are expensive and not widely available – for most activities carbohydrate (sugar)-only drinks would be just as beneficial.

FOODS AND DRINKS SUITABLE FOR CONSUMPTION DURING EXERCISE

Each of the following portions supply 30 g carbohydrate:

- 500 ml isotonic sports drink (6 g/100 ml)
- 250 ml energy drink (12 g/100 ml)
- 250 ml fruit juice mixed with 250 ml water
- 45 g cereal bar (1 or 1½ bars)
- 40 g raisins
- 1–2 bananas (200 g)
- 1 sachet energy gel (30 g).

How much should I drink during exercise?

During exercise, drinking water or a carbohydrate-containing drink will help offset your fluid (sweating) losses and prevent dehydration. Losing up to 2 per cent of your body weight (e.g. 1.2 kg for a person weighing 60 kg) will probably not affect your performance, but greater losses will result in a drop in stamina, increased fatigue and light-headedness.

Exactly how much you need to drink depends on how heavily you are sweating. Clearly, the more you sweat, the more you need to drink. For most regular exercisers, drinking enough fluid to avoid dehydration is a common problem, hence the general advice to 'drink as much as possible'. However, the International Association

of Athletic Federations (IAAF) cautions against over-drinking during activities lasting longer than four hours. It advises drinking only when you're thirsty and opting for a sports drink (containing carbohydrate and sodium) rather than plain water, in order to prevent hyponataemia (water intoxication).

For most types of vigorous activity, fluid losses typically amount to between 500ml and 1 litre per hour, more in hot or humid conditions. If you plan to exercise for longer than an hour, drinking 500 ml to one litre of a sports drink (or diluted fruit juice) would be a realistic target, and would reduce your risk of dehydration. If you exercise for a shorter time or at a lower intensity, drink proportionally less – the risk of dehydration would be smaller. As a rule of thumb, opt for a sugar-containing drink (around 6 g/100 ml) during activities lasting longer than an hour, and water or more dilute drinks for shorter workouts.

When should I eat after exercising?

There is a two-hour window after exercising when the body is able to make glycogen significantly faster than normal. This slows over the subsequent four hours and thereafter returns to the normal rate. During this post-exercise period, cell membranes are more permeable and glucose is transported from the bloodstream across the muscle cell membrane more readily, so more glucose can be converted into glycogen.

Clearly, the sooner you can consume carbohydrate after your workout, the quicker your body will recover. This is particularly important if you work out daily. In practice, try to have a carbohydrate-rich drink or snack (see below) as soon as possible after your workout – ideally within 30 minutes and no later than two hours. However, if you plan to leave more than 24 hours between your workouts, the exact timing of your post-exercise meal is a little less crucial. Provided you consume enough carbohydrate to refuel your glycogen stores, you need not be too concerned about refuelling in the first two hours.

What should I eat after exercising?

Clearly, after exercise you need to consume carbohydrate to replace the fuel (glycogen) you have just burned. For serious exercisers, the IAAF recommends consuming 1 g of carbohydrate per kg of body weight during the two-hour post-exercise period. For example, a person weighing 60 kg should consume 60 g carbohydrate. Thereafter, you should aim to consume around 50 g carbohydrate every two hours, or until your next main meal.

Both serious and recreational exercisers would benefit from a carbohydrate-rich snack or meal eaten as soon as practical following your workout. Ideally, this should include some protein as well as carbohydrate. This type of meal has been shown to promote faster recovery of glycogen stores and muscle tissue compared with a carbohydrate-only meal. It causes a greater rise in insulin levels, which helps the muscle cells take up glucose and amino acids from the bloodstream. It also lowers cortisol levels, which means less muscle breakdown after intense exercise.

Studies from the University of Texas have found that consuming food or drink containing carbohydrate and protein in the ratio of 3:1 immediately after exercise increases glycogen storage by 38 per cent. Faster glycogen refuelling means speedier recovery. A 2007 study at Loughborough and Bath Universities showed that runners could run longer following a four-hour recovery period during which they consumed a carbohydrate-protein drink. This also helps reduce muscle damage and muscle soreness, and promotes muscle repair, according to a 2007 review of studies carried out by researchers at Maastricht University.

You'll find various commercial recovery drinks containing carbohydrate and protein, but it may be more economical to opt for real foods and drinks. Try skimmed milk or flavoured milk – according to researchers at Loughborough University, skimmed chocolate milk improved endurance more than conventional sports drinks. Other suitable recovery foods are shown in the boxes below.

High or low GI after exercise?

Immediately after exercise, opt for a moderate- to high-GI snack or drink to deliver carbohydrate and protein to your fuel-depleted muscles. Try rice cakes with peanut butter, a handful of dried fruit and nuts or a pot of yoghurt. When it comes to your day-to-day diet, opt for low-GI meals based on low-GI carbohydrates (*see* page 20), lean protein sources, vegetables and 'good' fats. Researchers at Loughborough

University have found that eating low-GI meals during the 24 hours following exercise improves endurance during your next workout. What's more, in their 2007 study, athletes consuming a low-GI recovery diet burned more fat and less glycogen than those consuming high-GI meals. It is possible, then, that a low-GI daily diet may help shed surplus body fat as well as improve your performance.

REFUELLING SNACKS

To be eaten within two hours after exercise.

- Fresh fruit and a glass of milk
- One or two cartons of low-fat fruit yoghurt
- A smoothie – whizz fresh fruit and yoghurt in a blender
- A homemade milkshake
- A yoghurt drink
- Flavoured milk
- A cereal bar with a milky drink
- A tuna, peanut butter or cheese sandwich
- A handful of dried fruit and nuts
- A few rice cakes with peanut butter or hummus
- A bowl of porridge made with skimmed milk
- Jacket potato with baked beans.

REFUELLING MEALS

- Noodles and vegetable stir-fry with turkey or cashew nuts
- Pasta with tomato pasta sauce, grilled fish *or* grated cheese with vegetables
- Jacket potato, chicken breast baked in foil, broccoli and carrots
- Bean and vegetable hotpot with wholegrain bread
- Rice with grilled turkey and steamed vegetables
- Lasagne or vegetable lasagne with salad
- Fish pie with vegetables
- Chilli or vegetarian chilli with rice and vegetables
- Dahl (lentils) with rice and vegetables
- Chicken curry with rice and vegetables
- Mashed or baked potato with grilled salmon and salad.

If I don't feel hungry after training, should I force myself to eat?
High-intensity endurance training, particularly in warm conditions, can sometimes suppress your post-workout appetite. This is because more of your blood flow is concerned with your exercising muscles, so the hunger signals your brain receives from your gut sensors are weaker. If the thought of eating straight after a workout makes you feel queasy, try liquid meals such as smoothies, yoghurt drinks, flavoured milk or milkshakes.

Carbohydrate

How much carbohydrate should I eat each day?
There's no doubt that carbohydrate is very important for endurance exercise. A high consumption produces high levels of muscle and liver glycogen, which, according to numerous studies, promote a greater endurance capacity and better performance. On the other hand, a low carbohydrate intake produces low glycogen levels, early fatigue and diminished endurance. So, for practically all activities, high pre-exercise glycogen levels will help to improve your endurance, delay exhaustion, and help you exercise longer and harder.

Previously, scientists talked about carbohydrate intakes in terms of percentages – for example, the International Conference on Foods, Nutrition and Performance in 1991 recommended a diet containing 60–70 per cent of energy from carbohydrate. But this method is not very user-friendly as most people cannot calculate easily the percentage of carbohydrate energy they eat. It is also misleading as it assumes an optimal energy intake. For example, those with very high or low energy intakes may not consume optimal amounts of carbohydrate.

Nowadays, scientists prefer calculating carbohydrate requirements from a person's body weight and training volume, since your glycogen storage capacity is roughly proportional to body weight. The greater your body weight, the greater your muscle mass and therefore the greater your glycogen storage capacity. Also, the longer and harder you train, the more glycogen (carbohydrate) you need to fuel your muscles.

Table 1.2, 'How much carbohydrate do I need?', indicates the amount of carbohydrate you need per kg of body weight for different activity levels. Most people who exercise at low or moderate intensities for up to two hours daily require about 5–7 g per kg body weight; but, during periods of heavy training, requirements may increase to 7–10 g per kg body weight.

For example, for a 60 kg athlete exercising one to two hours a day:

Carbohydrate needs = 6–7 g/kg of body weight
= (60 × 6) to (60 × 7)
= 360 to 420 g per day

The heavier you are, and the more active you are, the more carbohydrate you will need to maintain your muscle glycogen stores.

Table 1.2 How much carbohydrate do I need?

Number of hours of exercise per day	g carbohydrate per kg body weight per day	g carbohydrate per day for a 60 kg person
0–1	5–6	300–360
1–2	6–7	360–420
3–4	7–8	420–480
4+	8–10	480–600

If I overeat carbohydrate, will I gain weight?

It can be tricky to judge exactly how much food to eat. If you fail to consume enough carbohydrate you risk compromising your performance, but if you eat too much, you may put on unwanted pounds. There is a maximum level of carbohydrate that can be stored as glycogen in your liver and your muscles: roughly 100 g glycogen (equivalent to 400 kilocalories) in your liver, and 400 g glycogen (equivalent to 1600 kilocalories) in your muscles (although the more muscle you have, the more glycogen can be stored). After exercise, when glycogen stores are depleted, carbohydrate in your food will be converted preferentially into glycogen. But only 25–35 g carbohydrates per hour can be turned into glycogen. Eat too much too soon and the resulting 'overspill' will be converted into fat. So keep a check on portion sizes and avoid too many high-GI carbohydrates, which convert rapidly into blood glucose.

Which are better for performance – simple or complex carbohydrates?

The terms 'simple' and 'complex' refer to the size of the molecules (i.e. the number of sugar units they contain). Simple carbohydrates comprise a single sugar (e.g. glucose) or two linked sugar units (e.g. sucrose). 'Complex' carbohydrates contain anywhere between two and several thousand sugar units. They include starch (found in potatoes and cereals, for example) and fibre (found in fruit, vegetables and whole grains).

The problem with this classification system is that it tells you little about the effects of that food on your blood glucose level. It is a myth that complex carbohydrates provide 'slow-release' energy or simple carbohydrates provide 'fast-release' energy. In many cases, the opposite is true. For example, white bread (which contains complex carbohydrates) produces a rapid blood sugar rise, while apples (containing simple carbohydrates) produce a gradual blood sugar rise. Nowadays, carbohydrates are more commonly categorised according to their glycaemic index (GI).

What exactly is the GI?

The glycaemic index (GI) was developed by David Jenkins in 1982. He discovered that, contrary to popular belief, many starchy foods affected blood glucose levels quite dramatically, while some sugary foods had little effect.

The GI is a ranking of foods from 0 to 100 based on their immediate effect on blood sugar levels. It's a measure of how quickly the food turns into glucose in the bloodstream. In this system, all foods are compared with a reference food (normally glucose), which has a GI of 100, and are tested in equivalent carbohydrate amounts. To measure the GI of a food, volunteers are given portions of food containing 50 g carbohydrate and the rise in blood glucose is then measured over the next two hours, compared with glucose. Foods that produce a similar blood sugar rise to glucose would get a high-GI score; foods that produce a relatively small rise in blood sugar would get a low-GI score.

Foods with a high GI (above 70) cause a rapid rise in blood sugar levels. These include most refined starchy foods – potatoes, cornflakes, white bread and white rice – as well as sugary foods such as soft drinks, biscuits and sweets.

Foods with a low GI (below 55) produce a slower and smaller blood sugar rise. These include beans, lentils, coarse-grain breads, muesli, fruit and dairy products. Foods that contain no carbohydrate – meat, fish, chicken, eggs, oil, butter and margarine – have no GI value.

What affects the GI value of a food?

There are several things. First, the presence of fat and protein in the food slows the absorption of carbohydrate. This helps to explain why chocolate, which is high in fat, has a low GI value. It also explains why spreading bread with butter lowers its GI value.

How you cook a food, the degree of processing and the ripeness of a fruit also affect its GI. Even the structure of the carbohydrate itself influences the GI. For example, processed instant oats have a higher GI than traditional rolled oats used to make porridge. This is because, as a result of the processing, the starch in instant oats is more easily exposed to digestive enzymes, causing it to break down and enter the bloodstream more rapidly.

Meanwhile, some foods have low GI values because they are packed with fibre, which acts as a physical barrier, slowing down the absorption of carbohydrate into the blood.

So what happens when I eat a meal?

The GI only tells you about the effect of a particular food on blood glucose levels when it is eaten on its own. But when you eat a mixture of foods together, as in a meal, the GI value of that whole meal changes. As a guideline, though, the more low-GI foods you include in a meal, the lower the overall GI value of that meal will be.

Are there any drawbacks to the GI?

As outlined above, one of the main limitations to GI diets is the fact that it is difficult to calculate the GI value of a whole meal. Meanwhile, some foods with a high level of fat have a low GI, which gives a falsely favourable impression of them. Chocolate and crisps, for example, are high in fat and contain few vitamins and

Table 1.3 The glycaemic index (GI) of foods

Low GI (<55)		Moderate GI (56–69)		High GI (>70)	
Peanuts	14	Potato (boiled, old)	56	White bread	70
Fructose	19	Sultanas	56	Isostar	70
Cherries	22	Power bar	56	Golden Grahams	71
Grapefruit	25	Pitta bread	57	Millet	71
Lentils (red)	26	Apricots	57	Wholemeal bread	71
Whole milk	27	Porridge	58	Water biscuit	71
Chickpeas	28	Basmati rice	58	Bagel	72
Red kidney beans	28	Squash (diluted)	58	Breakfast cereal bar (e.g. Crunchy Nut Cornflakes)	72
Lentils (green/brown)	30	Digestive biscuits	59	Watermelon	72
Butter beans	31	Pineapple	59	Cheerios	74
Apricot (dried)	31	Just Right cereal	60	Bran flakes	74
Meal replacement bar	31	Pizza	60	Mashed potato	74
Skimmed milk	32	Ice cream	61	Chips	75
Protein shake	32	Sweet potato	61	Rice cakes	78
Fruit yoghurt (low fat)	33	Muesli bar	61	Gatorade	78
Chocolate milk	34	Tortillas/corn chips	63	Cornflakes	81
Custard	35	White rice	64	Rice Krispies	82
Plain yoghurt (low fat)	36	Rye crispbread	64	Baked potato	85
Spaghetti	38	Shortbread	64	French baguette	95
Apples	38	Raisins	64	Lucozade™	95
Tinned peaches (in fruit juice)	38	Couscous	65		
Pear	38	Cantaloupe melon	65		
Yoghurt drink	38	Mars bar	65		
Protein bar	38	Instant porridge	66		
Plum	39	Croissant	67		
Apple juice	40	Sustain	68		
Strawberries	40	Fanta™	68		
All Bran	42	Sucrose	68		
Orange	42	Weetabix	74		
Peach	42	Shredded wheat	75		
Milk chocolate	43				
Muffin (apple)	44				
Sponge cake	46				
Grapes	46				
Pineapple juice	46				
Macaroni	47				

Low GI (<55)		Moderate GI (56–69)	High GI (>70)
Carrots	47		
Bulgar wheat	48		
Peas	48		
Baked beans	48		
Muesli	49		
Boiled potato	50		
Rye bread	50		
Mango	51		
Strawberry jam	51		
Banana	52		
Orange juice	52		
Kiwi fruit	53		
Buckwheat	54		
Sweetcorn	54		
Crisps	54		
Muesli (e.g. Alpen)	55		
Honey	55		
Brown rice	55		

Source: Foster-Powell *et al.*, 2002. Adapted with permission from the *American Journal of Clinical Nutrition* © Am. J. Clin. Nutr. American Society for Nutrition.

minerals, yet they have a low GI. The GI also doesn't take account of the portion size eaten. For example, watermelon, with its high GI (72), is off the menu on a low-GI diet. But an average portion (120 g), containing just 6 g carbohydrate, doesn't raise your blood glucose level significantly. You would need to eat several slices (720 g) to obtain 50 g carbohydrate – the amount used in the GI test.

Is a low-GI diet healthier?

A 2008 study by Australian researchers, analysing the diets of nearly 2 million people around the world, found that a high-GI diet increased the risk of diabetes, heart disease, stroke and various cancers. Studies at Harvard University in the USA have correlated a low risk of diseases such as heart disease and diabetes with a low-GI diet. In other words, people who eat lots of low-GI foods such as whole grains, pulses, fruit and vegetables tend to be the healthiest. But that's not too surprising as a low-GI diet is in line with general healthy advice to eat more fibre, and less saturated fat and sugar.

Protein

Why do I need protein?

Protein is needed for the growth, formation and repair of body cells. It forms part of the structure of every cell in your body, including muscle, skin, hair and nails. It is also needed for making enzymes, hormones and antibodies. Your body can't store protein, so it must be supplied on a daily basis from the foods you eat.

What are amino acids?

Amino acids are the small building blocks of proteins. There are 20 different amino acids that, in different combinations, make up thousands of proteins. A protein can consist of between 50 and tens of thousands of amino acids, linked together. Eight amino acids must be provided by the diet (the 'essential amino acids'), while the others can be made by the body. For your body to use food proteins properly, all eight essential amino acids have to be present. Animal proteins, as well as soya and Quorn, contain all eight essential amino acids, but plant proteins (pulses, cereals, nuts) contain fewer, so these need to be combined (e.g. beans on toast, lentils and rice, peanut butter on bread) to give the full complement of amino acids. The general rule of thumb is to have grains and pulses or nuts and grains together.

How much protein should I eat?

Athletes have higher protein requirements than non-active people, to compensate for the increased muscle breakdown that occurs during and after intense exercise, as well as to build new muscle cells. Endurance athletes require between 1.2 and 1.4 g protein per kg body weight per day. That's 72–84 g daily for a 60 kg woman. Strength athletes require 1.4–1.7 g per kg body weight per day, or 84–102 g daily. The GDA for the general population is 45 g for women and 55 g for men. Women generally need less than men due to their smaller size. Most people eat more protein than they actually need, so deficiencies are rare and protein supplements are not normally necessary – you can get the necessary levels of protein from a balanced diet.

What happens if I don't get enough protein?

If you don't eat enough protein for a few days or weeks the body will simply adapt to a lower intake by 'recycling' existing proteins into new ones. However, if you were to continue eating a low-protein diet for several months, you may develop symptoms of protein deficiency: wasting and shrinkage of muscle tissue, oedema (build-up of fluids, particularly in the feet and ankles), anaemia and slow growth (in children). This condition is very rare in the West (even among vegetarians and vegans), but common in developing countries.

Is too much protein harmful?

Some athletes eat high-protein diets in the belief that extra protein leads to increased strength and muscle mass. But this isn't true – it is stimulation of muscle tissue through exercise, not extra protein, that leads to muscle growth. Extra protein is unlikely to be harmful; it will be broken down into urea (which is excreted) and fuel, which is either used for energy or stored as fat if your calorie intake exceeds your output. Contrary to popular belief, there's no evidence that high protein intakes damage the kidneys or liver in healthy people.

Which are healthier – animal or vegetable proteins?

Animal protein sources (poultry, fish, meat, dairy products and eggs) generally provide a higher concentration of protein than vegetable sources (beans, lentils, nuts, grains, soya, Quorn). They also contain all eight essential amino acids, whereas plant proteins may lack certain essential amino acids, making them less readily absorbed. However, this isn't necessarily a problem: eating a mixture of plant protein sources (such as beans on toast) enhances amino acid absorption.

Animal protein sources contain no fibre, and some foods (e.g. meat and full-fat dairy products) may also contain high levels of saturated fat. Swapping some animal protein for vegetable protein is a good way to lower your saturated fat intake and boost your intake of fibre. High intakes of animal protein increase acidity in the bloodstream, which is associated with increased bone mineral loss and osteoporosis risk. Substituting vegetable for animal protein will help cut your risk of this.

Can vegetarian athletes get enough protein?

A number of studies have concluded that most athletes are able to meet their protein needs from a vegetarian diet as long as a variety of protein-rich foods are consumed and energy intakes are adequate. Contrary to popular belief, even strength athletes can obtain enough protein from a vegetarian diet – the limiting factor for muscle mass gains appears to be total caloric intake, not protein intake.

Most foods contain at least some protein. If you omit meat and fish then you need to substitute a plant protein – for example, beans, lentils, nuts, seeds, dairy products, eggs, soya products (tofu, soya milk, soya 'yoghurt', soya mince), cereals or Quorn. The protein content of various foods is shown in Table 1.4. Single plant foods do not contain all the essential amino acids you need in the right proportions, but when you mix plant foods together, any deficiency in one is cancelled out by any excess in the other. This is called **protein complementing**. Combining grains and pulses, such as rice and beans, increases the overall levels of amino acids, which is just as good as, if not better than, sourcing protein from animal foods. A few examples of such combinations are beans on toast, muesli, and rice and lentils. Including dairy products or eggs as well adds the missing amino acids (e.g. macaroni cheese, quiche, porridge). Examples of other protein combinations include:

- tortilla or wrap filled with refried beans
- bean and vegetable hotpot with rice or pasta
- Quorn chilli with rice
- peanut butter sandwich
- lentil soup with a roll
- Quorn korma with naan bread
- stir-fried tofu and vegetables with rice
- tofu burger in a roll.

In essence, you can achieve protein complementation by combining plant foods from two or more of the following categories.

1. Pulses: beans, lentils, peas.
2. Grains: bread, pasta, rice, oats, breakfast cereals, corn, rye.
3. Nuts and seeds: peanuts, cashews, almonds, sunflower seeds, sesame seeds, pumpkin seeds.
4. Quorn and soya products: soya milk, tofu, tempeh (fermented soya curd, similar to tofu but with a stronger flavour), soya mince, soya burgers, Quorn mince, Quorn fillets, Quorn sausages.

It is now known that the body has a pool of amino acids so that, if one meal is deficient, the shortfall can be made up from the body's own stores. Because of this, you don't have to worry about complementing amino acids all the time, as long as your diet is generally varied and well balanced. Even those foods not considered high in protein are adding some amino acids to this pool.

Table 1.4 The protein content of selected foods

Food	Protein (g)
Meat and fish	
1 lean fillet steak (105 g)	31
1 chicken breast fillet (125 g)	30
2 slices turkey breast (40 g)	10
1 salmon fillet (150 g)	30
Tuna, canned in brine	24
Dairy products	
1 slice (40 g) Cheddar cheese	10
2 tablespoons (112 g) cottage cheese	15
1 glass (200 ml) skimmed milk	7
1 glass (200 ml) soya milk	7
1 carton yoghurt (150 g)	6
1 egg (size 2)	8
Nuts and seeds	
1 handful (50 g) peanuts	12
1 tablespoon (20 g) peanut butter	5
Pulses	
1 small tin (205 g) baked beans	10
3 tablespoons (120 g) cooked lentils	9
3 tablespoons (120 g) cooked red kidney beans	10
Soya and Quorn products	
1 tofu burger (60 g)	5
1 Quorn burger (50 g)	6
Grains and cereals	
2 slices wholemeal bread	6
1 serving (230 g) cooked pasta	7

Fat

Why do I need fat in my diet?

Fat is a component of your body cell membranes, brain tissue, nerve sheaths and bone marrow, and cushions your organs. Fat in food also provides essential fatty acids (see below), as well as the fat-soluble vitamins A, D and E, and is an important source of energy (calories), providing nine calories per gram.

How much fat should I eat?

The International Olympic Committee (IOC) and IAAF have not set a target intake for fat: both focus on meeting carbohydrate and protein goals, with fat making up the calorie balance. In 2000, the American Dietetic Association and American College of Sports Medicine (ACSM) recommended a diet containing 20–25 per cent energy from fat, which is in line with the 33 per cent maximum advised by the UK Department of Health for the general population. A minimum of 15 per cent is recommended for optimum health.

In practice, you should aim to achieve a fat intake between 20 and 33 per cent of your calorie intake. So, for a female athlete consuming 2500 calories daily:

$$(2500 \times 20\%) \div 9 = 56 \text{ g}$$
$$(2500 \times 33\%) \div 9 = 94 \text{ g}$$

That is, between 56 and 94 g fat a day.

The Department of Health also recommends that no more than 10 per cent of energy should come from saturated fat; this means a daily maximum of 10 g for a female athlete consuming 2500 calories a day. Therefore, most of your fat intake should come from 'good', unsaturated fats, found in vegetable oils (e.g. olive, rapeseed, sunflower), nuts (all kinds), seeds (e.g. sunflower, sesame, pumpkin), oily fish (e.g. sardines, mackerel, salmon), peanut butter and avocado.

What's the difference between 'good' and 'bad' fats?

The term 'good' fats refers to unsaturated fats – monounsaturates and polyunsaturates – found in nuts, seeds, olives (and their oils) and fish. 'Bad' fats refers to saturated fats and trans fats, which have been linked to increased risk of heart disease and other degenerative illnesses.

Bad fats

Saturated fats are found in animal fats as well as products made with palm oil or palm kernel oil (a highly saturated fat). They have no beneficial role in keeping the body healthy – they raise blood cholesterol levels and increase the risk of heart disease – so you do not actually need any in your diet. However, it would be impractical to cut them out altogether, so stick to an intake less than the GDA: 30 g for men and 20 g for women.

Main sources include fatty meats, full-fat dairy products, butter, lard, palm oil and palm kernel oil (both labelled as 'vegetable fat' on foods), some types of margarine and spreads, biscuits, cakes and desserts made with palm or palm kernel oil or 'vegetable fat'.

Trans fats are even more harmful than saturated fats. Very small amounts occur naturally in meat and dairy products, but most are formed artificially during the commercial process of hydrogenation, which converts unsaturated oils into solid spreads and shortenings (hydrogenated fats or oils). These hardened fats increase the shelf life of foods; they are cheap and help give foods such as biscuits desirable properties such as crispiness.

The problem with trans fats is that they increase LDL (low-density lipoprotein) cholesterol ('bad' cholesterol) levels and lower HDL (high-density lipoprotein or 'good' cholesterol) levels, and harden and stiffen the arteries, which increases the risk of heart disease. Intakes greater than 5 g per day have been linked to a 30 per cent increased risk of heart disease, as well as a greater risk of diabetes, allergies and certain cancers.

Clearly, you should try to avoid these fats completely – the Food Standards Agency (FSA) recommends a maximum daily intake of 4–5 g per day. Avoid foods that have hydrogenated oils and partially hydrogenated oils on the ingredients list.

Table 1.5 Good and bad fats

Good fats	Bad fats
Monounsaturated fats: olive oil, rapeseed oil, avocados, nuts, peanut butter *Polyunsaturated fats:* sunflower oil, corn oil, sunflower margarine, nuts, seeds *Omega-3 fats:* sardines, salmon, mackerel, pilchards, walnuts, pumpkin seeds, omega-3 eggs	*Saturated fats:* fatty meats, burgers, sausages, butter, palm oil, biscuits, cakes, cheese *Trans fats:* some margarines and spreads, biscuits, pastries, pies, cakes, takeaway fried food

Good fats

Monounsaturated fats help lower 'bad' LDL cholesterol levels while maintaining levels of 'good' HDL, which helps cut heart disease and cancer risk. The Department of Health recommends an intake of up to 12 per cent of total calories. They're found in olive oil, rapeseed and soya oil, avocados, nuts, peanut butter and seeds.

Polyunsaturated fats include omega-3 and omega-6 fats. The average person eats 10 times more omega-6s than omega-3s, while a ratio of 5:1 or less would be a healthier balance.

Omega-3 fatty acids include alpha-linolenic acid (ALA), found in walnuts, pumpkin seeds, flax seeds and rapeseed oil, eicosapentanoic acid (EPA) and docosahexanoic acid (DHA), the latter two are both found only in oily fish (sardines, mackerel, salmon, fresh tuna, trout and herring). EPA and DHA are needed for the proper functioning of the brain; they protect against heart disease and stroke by reducing blood viscosity, and may help prevent memory loss and treat depression. They are important for female athletes as they help increase the delivery of oxygen to muscles, improve endurance, speed recovery, and reduce inflammation and joint stiffness. The minimum requirement is 0.9 g a day, which you can get from one portion (140 g) of oily fish a week or one tablespoon of omega-3-rich oil daily.

Omega-6 fatty acids include linolenic acid and gamma linolenic acid (GLA), found in sunflower, safflower, corn, groundnut and olive oils, peanuts and peanut butter, evening primrose oil, sunflower and sesame seeds. These oils are widely used in food manufacturing. For this reason, it's relatively easy to eat plenty of omega-6s, but most people aren't getting enough omega-3s. This can result in an imbalance of prostaglandins (responsible for controlling blood clotting, inflammation and the immune system).

Vitamins and minerals

Why do I need vitamins and minerals?

Vitamins and minerals are substances that are needed in tiny amounts to enable your body to work properly and prevent illness. Vitamins support the immune system, help the brain function properly and assist in converting food into energy. They are important for healthy skin and hair, controlling growth and balancing hormones. Some vitamins – the B vitamins and vitamin C – must be provided by the diet each day, as they cannot be stored. Minerals are needed for structural and regulatory functions, including bone strength, haemoglobin manufacture, fluid balance and muscle contraction.

What are RDAs?

The recommended daily amounts (RDAs) listed on food and supplement labels are rough estimates of nutrient requirements, set by the EU and designed to cover the needs of the majority of a population. The amounts are designed to prevent deficiency symptoms, and allow for a little storage as well as covering differences in needs from one person to the next. They are not targets; rather they are guides to help you check that you are probably getting enough nutrients.

Do female athletes need extra vitamins and minerals?

Your needs for many vitamins and minerals are higher than those of non-active women.

Regular, intense exercise increases your requirement for those micronutrients involved in energy metabolism, tissue growth and repair, red blood cell manufacture and free radical defence.

It is tempting to think that supplements are needed, but, in fact, there is little scientific evidence to suggest that supplements benefit performance. The consensus of opinion among researchers is that a balanced diet providing sufficient calories should provide all the vitamins and minerals athletes need to keep healthy and train hard. Indeed, diets naturally rich in vitamins and minerals, and antioxidants in particular, lessen the risks of heart disease and cancer. However, there's scant proof that vitamins in pills give the same benefits.

A review by the US Preventive Services Task Force in 2003 concluded that while multivitamins are generally harmless and useful for filling the gaps in your diet, there's no scientific evidence that they will reduce your risk of chronic diseases. According to a 2002 Harvard University study, supplementation can't erase the effects of a poor diet and a sedentary lifestyle. Foods contain additional important components such as fibre, phytonutrients and essential fatty acids.

How much is too much?

It's virtually impossible to overdose on vitamins and minerals from food. Problems of toxicity are more likely to arise from the use of supplements, so it is important to check the guidelines on the label and the safe upper levels (SULs) set by the FSA. The SUL is the amount that's unlikely to be harmful taken over a lifetime. In particular, the FSA warns against high doses of vitamin A (particularly for pregnant women, where high doses over prolonged periods of time can cause liver damage and birth defects in babies), vitamin B6, chromium picolinate, more than 1000 mg vitamin C daily, more than 17 mg iron daily, and vitamin D.

If I decide to take a supplement, what should I look for?

If you want to add multivitamins and minerals to your diet, look carefully at the label. Here are some guidelines to help you choose.

- It should contain around 23 key vitamins and minerals.
- The amounts of each vitamin should be between 100 and 1000 per cent of the RDA stated on the label, but below the SUL.
- The amounts of each mineral should be no higher than the RDA because higher doses may be toxic.
- Choose multivitamins containing beta-carotene rather than vitamin A – it is a more powerful antioxidant and, unlike vitamin A, is unlikely to have harmful side-effects in high doses.
- Avoid supplements with unnecessary ingredients such as sweeteners, colours, artificial flavours and talc (a bulking agent).

Table 1.6 A guide to vitamins and minerals

Vitamin/mineral	How much?*	Why is it needed?	What happens if you get too little?	What are the best food sources?	Side-effects of excessive intake
Vitamin A	700 mcg (men) 600 mcg (women) No SUL FSA recommends 1500 mcg max	Needed for growth and development in children; helps vision in dim light; keeps the skin, hair and eyes healthy; keeps the linings of organs such as the lungs and digestive tract healthy; helps the body to fight infections	Poor vision, dry skin, impaired growth in children, and an increased susceptibility to infection	Liver, cheese, oily fish, eggs, butter, margarine	Liver and bone damage; can harm unborn child in pregnant women (avoid during pregnancy)
Beta-carotene	No official RNI SUL = 7 mg	Converts into vitamin A, a powerful antioxidant that may protect against certain cancers and heart disease		Dark-green vegetables such as spinach and watercress, and yellow, orange and red fruits/vegetables such as carrots, tomatoes, dried apricots, sweet potatoes and mangoes	Excessive doses of beta-carotene can cause harmless orange tinge to skin; reversible

Vitamin/mineral	How much?*	Why is it needed?	What happens if you get too little?	What are the best food sources?	Side-effects of excessive intake
Thiamin	0.4 mg/1000 kcal 0.8 mg for women; 1 mg for men up to 50 years; 0.9 mg for men over 50 years No SUL FSA recommends 100 mg	Converts carbohydrate to energy; keeps nervous system and the heart healthy	Tiredness, poor appetite, headaches, muscle fatigue, poor concentration, depression, irritability and heart problems	Wholemeal bread, fortified breakfast cereals, nuts, pulses, meat	Excess is excreted so toxicity is rare
Riboflavin	1.3 mg (men) 1.1 mg (women) No SUL FSA recommends 40 mg	Converts carbohydrate, fat and protein into energy	Poor wound healing, and skin, eye and mouth problems such as watery, bloodshot eyes, flaky and dry skin, chapped lips and a sore tongue	Milk and dairy products, meat, eggs	Excess is excreted (producing yellow urine!) so toxicity is rare

Vitamin/mineral	How much?*	Why is it needed?	What happens if you get too little?	What are the best food sources?	Side-effects of excessive intake
Niacin	13 mg for women up to 50 years; 12 mg for women over 50 years; 17 mg for men up to 50 years; 16 mg for men over 50 years SUL = 17 mg	Converts carbohydrate, fat and protein into energy	Skin problems, weakness, fatigue and loss of appetite	Meat and offal, nuts, milk and dairy products, eggs, wholegrain cereals	Excess is excreted; high doses may cause hot flushes
Pantothenic acid	No RNI; a safe intake for adults is considered to be 3–7 mg	Releases energy from food, and keeps the nervous system and skin healthy	Deficiency very rare	Offal, fish, poultry, meat, whole grains, nuts, eggs, yoghurt, beans	Excess is excreted
Vitamin B6 (pyridoxine)	1.2 mg for women; 1.4 mg for adult men SUL = 80 mg	Metabolism of protein, fat and carbohydrate; essential for the formation of red blood cells, antibodies and brain chemicals called neurotransmitters	Deficiency rare	Liver, nuts, pulses, eggs, bread, cereals, fish, bananas	Very high doses (>2 g per day for a period of months) may cause nerve damage, including numbness in the hands and feet

Vitamin/mineral	How much?*	Why is it needed?	What happens if you get too little?	What are the best food sources?	Side-effects of excessive intake
Folic acid	200 mcg for women and men	Formation of red blood cells; works with vitamin B12 for growth and the reproduction of cells; good intakes when planning a pregnancy and in the first 12 weeks also protect against birth defects	Tiredness, apathy and depression; low intakes prior to and during the early stages of pregnancy may increase the risk of having a baby with a neural tube defect such as spina bifida or cleft palate	Dark-green leafy vegetables, oranges, fortified breakfast cereals and bread, yeast extract, nuts and pulses	May mask symptoms of a B12 deficiency
Vitamin C	40 mg SUL = 1000 mg	Formation of collagen, which constitutes connective tissue; needed for healthy bones, blood vessels, gums and teeth; promotes immune function; helps iron absorption	Loss of appetite, muscle cramps, dry skin, bleeding gums, bruising, nose bleeds, infections and poor wound healing; in severe cases scurvy develops	Fruit and vegetables (e.g. raspberries, blackcurrants, kiwi fruit, oranges, peppers, broccoli, cabbage, tomatoes)	Excess is excreted; doses over 2 g may lead to diarrhoea and excess urine formation; high doses (>2 g) may cause vitamin C to behave as a pro-oxidant (enhance free radical damage)

Vitamin/mineral	How much?*	Why is it needed?	What happens if you get too little?	What are the best food sources?	Side-effects of excessive intake
Vitamin D	No RNI for adults under 65; 10 mcg for adults over 65 SUL = 25 mcg	Needed for strong bones (with calcium and phosphorus); helps to absorb calcium; may help to prevent osteoporosis in later life	Reduced absorption of calcium; increased risk of osteoporosis	Sunlight, oily fish, eggs, liver, fortified breakfast cereals, margarine	Toxicity rare; very high doses may cause high blood pressure, irregular heartbeat, excessive thirst
Vitamin E	No RNI in UK 10 mg in EU SUL = 540 mg	Antioxidant that helps protect against heart disease; promotes normal cell growth and development	Deficiency is rare	Vegetable oils, margarine, oily fish, nuts, seeds, egg yolk, avocado	Toxicity is rare
Calcium	1000 mg (men) 700 mg (women) SUL = 1500 mg	Builds bone and teeth; helps blood clotting, nerve and muscle function	Increased risk of osteoporosis	Milk and dairy products, sardines, dark-green leafy vegetables, pulses, nuts and seeds	High intake may interfere with absorption of other minerals; take with magnesium and vitamin D
Iron	8.7 mg (men) 14.8 mg (women) SUL = 17 mg	Formation of red blood cells; oxygen transportation; prevents anaemia	Iron deficiency; anaemia	Meat and offal, wholegrain cereals, fortified breakfast cereals, pulses, green leafy vegetables	Constipation, stomach discomfort; avoid unnecessary supplementation – may increase free radical damage

Vitamin/mineral	How much?*	Why is it needed?	What happens if you get too little?	What are the best food sources?	Side-effects of excessive intake
Zinc	9.5 mg (men) 7.0 mg (women) SUL = 25 mg	Healthy immune system; wound healing; skin and cell growth	Loss of taste; frequent infections; poor wound healing	Eggs, wholegrain cereals, meat, milk and dairy products	Interferes with absorption of iron and copper
Magnesium	300 mg (men) 270 mg (women) SUL= 400 mg	Healthy bones; muscle and nerve function; cell formation	Weakness; irregular heart-beat; muscle cramps	Cereals, fruit, vegetables, milk	May cause diarrhoea
Potassium	3500 mg SUL = 3700 mg	Fluid balance; muscle and nerve function	Muscle weakness; disorientation; irritability	Fruit, vegetables, cereals	Excess is excreted
Selenium	75 mcg (men) 60 mcg (women) SUL = 350 mcg	Antioxidant that helps protect against heart disease and cancer	Reduced fertility; frequent infections	Nuts, cereals, vegetables, dairy products, meat, eggs	Nausea, vomiting, hair loss

Notes

1. mg = milligram (1000 mg = 1 gram)
2. mcg = microgram (1000 mcg = 1 mg)
3. SUL = safe upper limit recommended by the Expert Group on Vitamins and Minerals, an independent advisory committee to the Food Standards Agency (FSA).

* The amount needed is given as the reference nutrient intake (RNI) (Department of Health, 1991). This is the amount of a nutrient that should cover the needs of 97 per cent of the population. Athletes in hard training may need more.

What exactly are antioxidants?

Antioxidant nutrients include various vitamins (such as beta-carotene, vitamin C and vitamin E), minerals (such as selenium) and other plant compounds called phytonutrients. They are found mostly in fruit and vegetables, seed oils, nuts, whole grains, beans and lentils. In the body, antioxidants help prevent or reduce cell damage caused by oxidation, a process that damages cells in the body and has been linked to the development of cancer, heart disease, Alzheimer's disease and Parkinson's disease.

What are phytonutrients?

Phytonutrients are plant compounds that have particular health benefits. They include plant pigments (found in coloured fruit and vegetables) and plant hormones (found in grains, beans, lentils, soya products and herbs). Many phytonutrients work as antioxidants, while others influence enzymes (such as those that block cancer agents). It is thought that a diet rich in phytonutrients helps fight cancer, reduce inflammation, combat free radicals, lower cholesterol, reduce heart disease risk and boost immunity.

Will antioxidant supplements make me healthier?

Evidence suggests that antioxidant supplements don't work as well as the naturally occurring antioxidants in foods such as fruits and vegetables. For example, vitamin A (beta-carotene) has been associated with a reduced risk of certain cancers but an increase in others, such as lung cancer in smokers. A study examining the effects of vitamin E found that it didn't offer the same benefits when taken as a supplement. A well-balanced diet, which includes antioxidants from whole foods, is best. Your diet should include five daily portions of fruit and vegetables. If you decide to take a supplement, choose one that contains all nutrients at the recommended levels.

Will antioxidant supplements improve my performance?

On balance, athletes may gain health benefits from antioxidant supplements but the benefits for performance are less clear. Some studies indicate that supplements may improve recovery. For example, in 2001 researchers at Loughborough University found that daily vitamin C supplementation (200 mg) for two weeks reduced muscle soreness and improved recovery following intense exercise. A 2004 US study found that women who took an antioxidant supplement (vitamin E, vitamin C and selenium) before and after weight training had significantly less muscle damage. In 2006, researchers at the University of North Carolina, USA, found that vitamin C supplementation before and after resistance training reduced post-exercise muscle soreness and muscle damage, and promoted recovery. But a review of studies presented at the 2003 IOC Consensus Conference on Sports Nutrition concluded that there is limited evidence that antioxidant supplements improve performance. The reason for these conflicting results may be that different studies used different antioxidant combinations and doses, making it difficult to draw clear conclusions.

Whether or not you opt for supplements, aim to eat at least five portions of fruit and vegetables daily – the more intense the colour, the higher the antioxidant content

– as well as foods rich in essential fats (such as avocados, oily fish and pure vegetable oils) for their vitamin E content. Scientists at the American Institute for Cancer Research say that eating at least five portions of fruit and vegetables each day can prevent 20 per cent of all cancers. The Department of Health in the UK and the World Health Organization advise a minimum of 400 g, or five portions, of fruit and vegetables a day.

Key points

- You can estimate your calorie needs and basal metabolic rate using predictive equations that take account of your weight and daily activity level.
- Your muscles derive energy from carbohydrate, fat and protein during exercise but the proportions of these fuels will depend on the type, intensity and duration of your activity, how well conditioned or 'fit' you are, and what you have eaten beforehand.
- Ideally, you should have a low-GI meal approximately two to four hours before exercising.
- If you are exercising for more than 60 minutes, consuming an extra 30–60 g carbohydrate per hour may help delay fatigue and increase your endurance.
- For most regular exercisers, drinking enough fluid to avoid dehydration is a common problem, but the IAAF cautions against over-drinking during activities lasting longer than four hours.

- If you plan to exercise for longer than an hour, drinking 500 ml to one litre of a sports drink (or diluted fruit juice) would be a realistic target, and would reduce your risk of dehydration.
- For serious exercisers, the IAAF recommends consuming 1 g of carbohydrate per kg of body weight during the two-hour post-exercise period.
- Consuming food or drink containing carbohydrate and protein in the ratio of 3:1 immediately after exercise increases glycogen recovery.
- A high carbohydrate consumption produces high levels of muscle and liver glycogen, which promotes a greater endurance capacity and better performance.
- Most people who exercise at low or moderate intensities for up to two hours daily require about 5–7 g carbohydrate per kg of body weight; but during periods of heavy training, requirements may increase to 7–10 g per kg of body weight.
- Endurance athletes require between 1.2 and 1.4 g protein per kg of body weight per day. Strength athletes require 1.4–1.7 g per kg of body weight per day, or 84–102 g daily.
- You should aim to achieve a fat intake that is between 20 and 33 per cent of your calorie intake; most should come from unsaturated fats.
- The omega-3 fatty acids are important for female athletes as they help increase the delivery of oxygen to muscles, improve endurance, speed recovery, and reduce inflammation and joint stiffness. The minimum requirement is 0.9 g a day.
- Your needs for many vitamins and minerals are higher than those of non-active women, but there is little scientific evidence to suggest that supplements benefit performance.

02

EATING DISORDERS AND DISORDERED EATING IN FEMALE ATHLETES

Many female athletes are very careful about what they eat, and often experiment with different dietary programmes in order to improve their performance. However, there is a fine line between paying attention to detail and obsessive eating behaviour. The pressure to be thin or attain higher performance may make you develop eating habits that not only put your performance at risk but also endanger your health.

Eating disorders are a key component of the female athlete triad (*see* Figures 2.1 and 2.2), a term that describes three interrelated health conditions: low calorie intake (with or without eating disorders), amenorrhoea and bone loss. When all three occur together this represents a serious health risk to the athlete. It is estimated that as many as 30 per cent of female athletes in 'thin-build' sports suffer from the female athlete triad, although the exact number is not known.

Originally, the triad was represented as a triangle (Figure 2.1), but researchers now prefer to depict it as two triangles, which illustrate better the spectrum of the three interrelated sub-clinical conditions (Figure 2.2). Each component of the female athlete triad is represented as being on a continuum of severity.

Fig 2.1 The female athlete triad

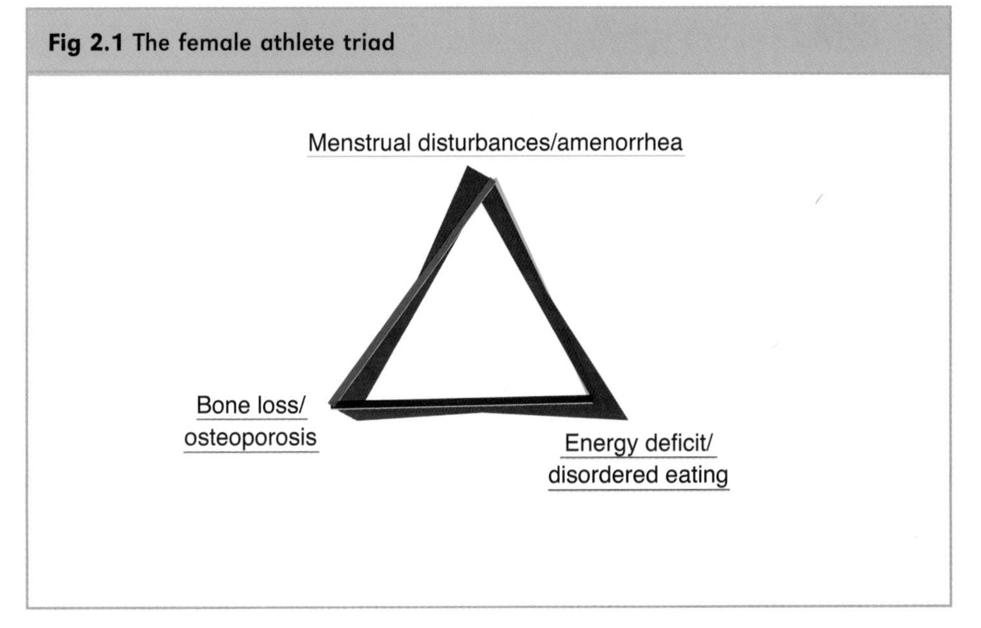

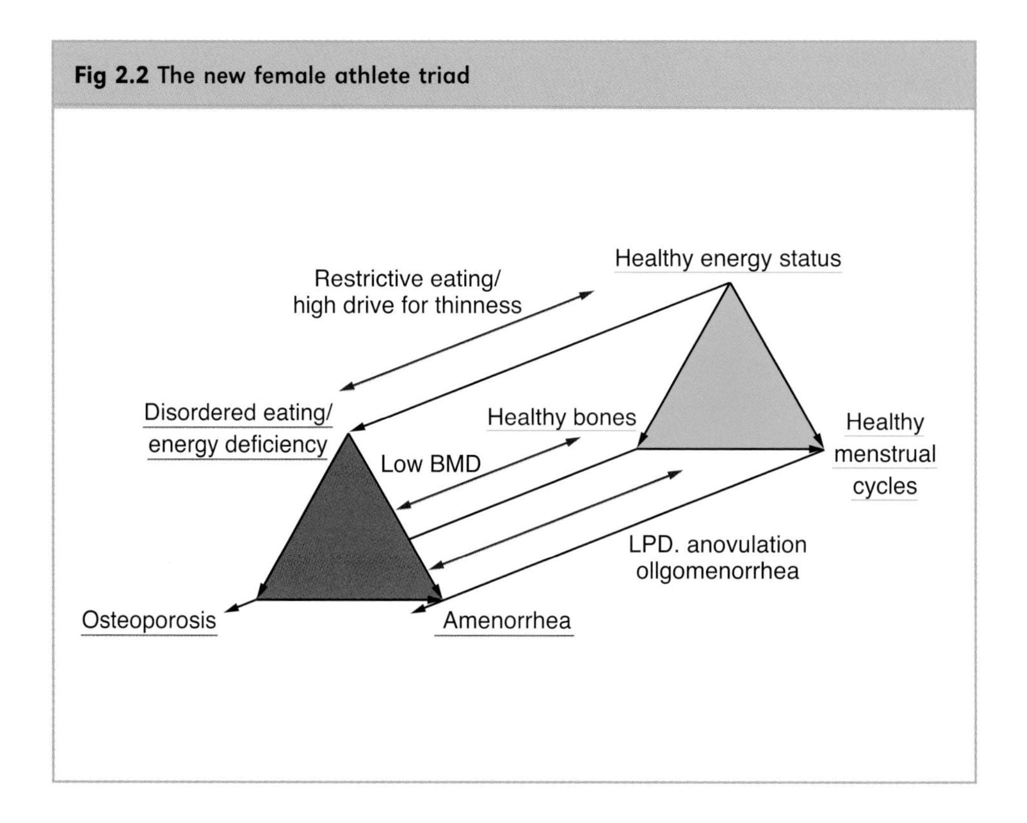

Fig 2.2 The new female athlete triad

The new female athlete triad highlights the fact that many athletes may not present with the extreme ends of the continuum, but rather may have 'sub-clinical' stages of one or more of the conditions, and that progression along the continuum of each component can occur at different rates. For example, an athlete may show signs of restrictive eating, but not meet the clinical criteria for an eating disorder. She may also display menstrual disturbances, such as a change in menstrual cycle length, but not yet have developed amenorrhea. Likewise, she may be losing bone, but may not yet have dropped below her age-matched normal range for bone density.

While the conditions represented by each continuum can occur independently of the other two conditions, it is more likely that, because of the clear associations between the three conditions, an athlete suffering from one element of the triad is also suffering from the others.

If you think you may have an eating disorder, or know someone who does, reading this chapter will help give you the information you need to make decisions and find support.

HOW COMMON ARE EATING DISORDERS?

Truly accurate data on the prevalence of eating disorders in the general population are not easy to come by since many sufferers are reluctant to admit to the problem. But beat, the eating disorders association, estimates that 1.15 million people in the UK have some form of eating disorder (undiagnosed or diagnosed). An NHS survey carried out in 2007 found that around one in five 16–25-year-old women showed signs of a problem with food.

WHAT IS THE DIFFERENCE BETWEEN ANOREXIA AND BULIMIA?

Anorexia is an eating behaviour characterised by self-starvation. Bulimia is a repeated cycle of overeating (bingeing) and then getting rid of the food before it can be digested (purging). These disorders are not just fads or bad habits – they are serious psychiatric illnesses that require medical, psychiatric or behavioural treatment.

How common are eating disorders and disordered eating among female athletes?

Many studies have attempted to measure the prevalence of disordered eating patterns in those taking part in sports and fitness activities, with estimates ranging from 1 to 60 per cent. This very wide range is due to differences in the design of the studies as well as differences in those taking part. Nevertheless, eating disorders and disordered eating are certainly more common among female athletes than the general population. And those competing in 'thin-build' sports (i.e. where a low body weight, body fat level or thin physique is perceived to be advantageous) are more prone to developing eating disorders than athletes competing in sports where these factors are considered less important. 'Thin-build' sports fall into four categories:

1. aesthetic sports that are judged subjectively (such as gymnastics, figure skating, ballet and synchronised swimming)
2. endurance sports, where a low body fat level aids speed and efficiency of movement (such as middle-distance and long-distance running)
3. weight division sports in which the athlete's weight determines the category they compete in (e.g. wrestling, karate and judo)
4. gym sports, which demand muscularity as well as low levels of body fat (such as bodybuilding and aerobics).

According to a 2001 study at the University of Leeds, UK, 16 per cent of elite female middle- and long-distance runners had anorexia or bulimia, compared with 1–2 per cent for the general population.

A 2004 study of 1620 male and female elite Norwegian athletes found that 42 per cent of women competing in aesthetic sports and 24 per cent of those competing in endurance events met the clinical criteria for an eating disorder. And, in a 2007 survey carried out at Coastal Carolina University, USA, 19 per cent of female cross-country runners reported having a current or previous eating disorder.

Women participating in gym sports are also vulnerable to eating disorders. A 1996 study by researchers at Auburn University at Montgomery, USA, found that 23 per cent of female aerobics instructors had a history of bulimia and 17 per cent had a history of anorexia. Women who work out in the gym or compete in bodybuilding also have a higher than average risk. According to a US study of female weight trainers and bodybuilders, many have a fear of becoming fat, are obsessed with food and weight, and use laxatives to lose weight. A 2006 Canadian study also showed that many bodybuilders are preoccupied with their weight and shape, binge regularly and have a high risk of bulimic behaviour.

But this may be only the tip of the iceberg. Other studies have revealed that many female athletes who don't meet the clinical criteria for an eating disorder nevertheless have unhealthy weight control behaviour and a poor body image. For example, in a 2002 study of 425 female athletes carried out at Ball State University, Indiana, USA, 32 per cent had disordered eating habits, compared with 5.6 per cent with a clinical eating disorder. A 2004 US study of elite female figure skaters found that 30 per cent considered themselves overweight, had a poor body image and indicated a preference for a thinner body shape. Their calorie intake was one-third lower than the recommended daily intake.

Aesthetic sports	Endurance sports and low weight performance sports	Weight division sports	Gym sports
Gymnastics Figure skating Ballet and dance Synchronised swimming	Middle- and long-distance running Cycling Swimming Horse racing	Lightweight rowing Judo Karate Wrestling Boxing	Bodybuilding Aerobics Fitness

Table 2.1 High-risk sports for eating disorders

What's the difference between an eating disorder and disordered eating?

Both these terms are often used interchangeably to describe restrictive or chaotic eating behaviours – but, in fact, they don't mean the same thing.

An eating disorder is a clinical condition defined by specific criteria set out in the American Psychiatric Association's (APA) Diagnostic and Statistical Manual of Mental Disorders (DSM–IV). The two most well-recognised forms are anorexia nervosa and bulimia nervosa. Anorexia nervosa is an extremely restrictive eating behaviour in which the individual continues to restrict food and feel fat in spite of being 15 per cent or more below an ideal body weight. Bulimia nervosa refers to a cycle of food restriction followed by bingeing and purging.

Disordered eating is a general term used to describe a wide range of abnormal and harmful eating behaviours that sufferers use to try to lose weight or maintain an abnormally low body weight. These may include limiting certain foods or food groups, severely restricting calorie intake, or occasional bingeing and purging. Sufferers have some but not all the characteristics of clinical eating disorders.

In all cases, sufferers tend to have a distorted body image and an unhealthy preoccupation with food. Eating behaviour is out of control. It's as much about attitude and behaviour towards food as it is about consumption of food.

What is anorexia nervosa?

Anorexia nervosa, commonly called anorexia, is a serious psychiatric condition. The word 'anorexia' literally means 'loss of appetite'. But anorexia nervosa is more like self-starvation – sufferers become so obsessed with losing weight and dieting that they ignore their body's hunger signals. People with anorexia deny their hunger, and strive to gain control and independence. In fact, denial and a desire for control are the two major features of the condition. As anorexia progresses, weight loss can become extreme, and sufferers often develop psychological and physical problems.

According to the DSM-IV criteria, anorexia is diagnosed in a person who:

- weighs at least 15 per cent less than the minimum average for his or her height, but has no physical illness causing the weight loss
- has an intense fear of gaining weight or 'becoming fat'
- has severe body dissatisfaction, and sees her or himself as 'fat' despite being underweight
- in a female, has amenorrhoea – the absence of at least three consecutive periods.

Sufferers are in continual pursuit of thinness and try to achieve this through self-starvation. Initially, they may have what appears to be a 'normal' desire to lose weight but, as dieting continues, they develop a more distorted body image, believing they are fat when they are severely underweight. The fear of fatness becomes an obsession and actually increases as they lose weight.

Many anorexics exercise excessively to burn off extra calories and avoid fatness. They find it very difficult to acknowledge their disorder and often withdraw socially, in part due to starvation and in part due to feelings of low self-worth.

Table 2.2 Characteristics and warning signs of anorexia nervosa

Characteristics	Warning signs
▪ Weight 15 per cent lower than minimum average for height ▪ Self-starvation ▪ Obsessive fear of weight gain ▪ Feeling fat when thin ▪ Low self-esteem ▪ Social withdrawal ▪ Distorted body image ▪ Obsessive exercise	▪ You have lost a lot of weight ▪ You feel fat even when you are thinner than other athletes ▪ You lie about what you have eaten to your family and friends ▪ You think about weight loss, food and your sport all the time ▪ Your periods have stopped, or never started ▪ You weigh yourself a lot and think that an extra pound will affect your performance ▪ You have difficulty sleeping ▪ You notice a layer of soft hair appearing all over your body

What are the warning signs of anorexia nervosa?

The most obvious warning signs are extreme thinness and weight loss. However, people with the disorder fiercely deny the condition and become very good at covering up the outward symptoms. So what other signs can you look for?

- People with anorexia are likely to feel cold much of the time, even in summer or in a warm room. As subcutaneous fat levels become low, it is difficult to maintain normal body temperature.
- They usually have a great interest in food and knowledge of calories. Many take great pleasure in preparing food for other people, but they eat very little themselves. Despite their interest in food, they feel very anxious around mealtimes and there may be frequent family arguments over food.
- Anorexics may often feel light-headed and dizzy. Severe dieting results in low blood glucose levels and also a drop in blood volume, causing low blood pressure. Starvation may affect the organs, including the heart. Many anorexics have a slow heartbeat.

- They may feel restless and tend to sleep very little, often waking early. Many are obsessed with weighing themselves. You may also notice an increased amount of facial and body hair.
- It's not unusual for anorexics to feel forgetful, irritable and unhappy. They may also experience sleeplessness, an inability to concentrate and feelings of hopelessness. These symptoms may progress to depression.

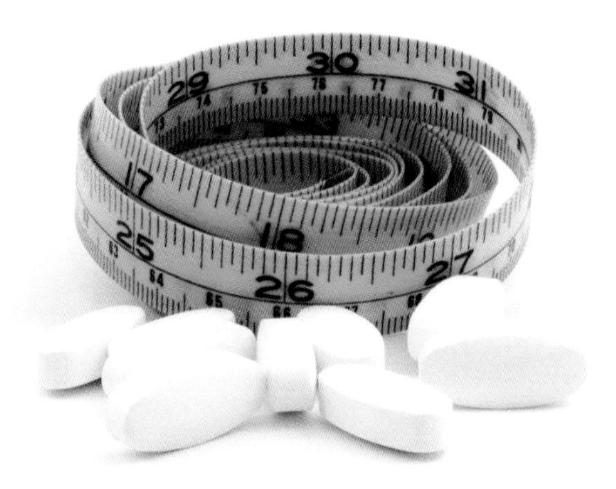

What is bulimia nervosa?

Bulimia literally means 'ox hunger' – a reference to the insatiable appetite that accompanies this disorder. People with bulimia tend to use extreme methods to lose weight, alternating between strict dieting and overeating.

Bulimia nervosa is characterised by repeated cycles of bingeing and purging. Bingeing means eating large amounts of food in a short period of time; bulimia sufferers will then compensate for the binge and try to get rid of the food to avoid gaining weight. Purging means getting rid of the food by self-induced vomiting, and/or abuse of laxatives, diet pills or diuretics. Instead of purging, some sufferers take excessive exercise.

The main features of bulimia nervosa, as defined by the DSM-IV criteria, are:

- episodes of binge eating followed by purging that have occurred at least twice a week for three months
- feeling out of control during the bingeing and purging episodes
- being dissatisfied with your body image.

Like anorexics, those with bulimia are driven by a desire to lose weight and attain thinness. They try to restrict their food intake, but lack the rigid self-control of anorexics, eventually succumbing to hunger and bingeing on vast amounts of food. A typical binge may contain up to 5000 calories, and a person with bulimia may binge once in a while or several times a day.

Many people struggle with their relationship with food, and may feel guilty or fearful around it. But someone with bulimia would also feel overly concerned with their weight, and confuse the sensation of hunger and strong emotions such as anxiety, fear or frustration. In other words, they experience these emotions as an urge to eat. Eating brings relief and comfort. They have a 'love/hate' relationship with food: on the one hand, they see food as a source of comfort, security and pleasure; while, on the other, they fear food will make them gain weight, thus it becomes a foe.

After a binge, people with bulimia feel guilt, shame and anxiety, and will then try to purge their body of the food by vomiting, exercising excessively or using laxatives or diuretics.

As with anorexia, many of the psychological characteristics precede or are exacerbated by the development of the disorder. These include low self-esteem, anxiety, depression, anger, a high need for approval, and body dissatisfaction.

Characteristics	Warning signs
■ Bingeing on large amounts of food ■ Guilt and remorse after bingeing ■ Purging ■ Starvation ■ Excessive exercise ■ Distorted body image ■ Obsession with food and weight	■ You regularly suffer from sore throats and experience infections ■ Your face appears puffy or swollen ■ Your periods are irregular ■ You are obsessed with losing weight ■ You make yourself sick after meals or take laxatives because you think they will help you lose weight ■ You eat in secret, and lie to your family and friends about your eating habits ■ You feel emotional and depressed, and have mood swings

What are the warning signs of bulimia?

Bulimia is difficult to diagnose because the problem is often hidden – someone with bulimia may not look any different from anyone else. They can be of normal weight, or even overweight. However, there are warning signs, such as frequent weighing (many will weigh themselves several times a day), puffy face, enamel erosion on the teeth, and marks on their fingertips or knuckles from self-induced vomiting. You may notice mood swings and changes in their eating behaviour. They may act differently from how they used to. They may disappear after meals to get rid of food, and go to the bathroom a lot to purge. You may find evidence of secretive eating, such as discarded food wrappers or large amounts of food disappearing from the fridge and kitchen – sufferers may buy, take or even steal large amounts of food; much of it tends to be snack food, which is eaten quickly and alone.

PERSONALITY CHARACTERISTICS OF BULIMIA NERVOSA

- Desire for thinness
- Low self-esteem
- High need for approval
- Impulsive
- Prone to anxiety, anger, depression

What is disordered eating?

Disordered eating is a broad term covering a wide range of abnormal and unhealthy eating behaviours that are used in an attempt to lose weight or maintain an extremely low body weight. It is not a clinical eating disorder as it does not meet the DSM-IV criteria for an eating disorder, but it may include some of the major characteristics of anorexia or bulimia. It is often referred to as a sub-clinical eating disorder.

People with disordered eating have an intense fear of gaining weight or becoming fat, even though their weight is normal, or even below normal. They are preoccupied with food and calories, and have a distorted body image. They attempt to lose

HAVE YOU GOT AN EATING PROBLEM?

This questionnaire is not intended as a diagnostic method for eating problems nor as a substitute for a full diagnosis by an eating disorders specialist.

- Do you exercise *specifically* to lose weight or body fat?
- Do you worry about or dislike your body shape?
- Do you often feel 'fat' one day and 'thin' the next?
- Do your friends and family insist that you are slim while you feel fat?
- Do you feel guilty after eating a high-calorie or high-fat meal?
- Do you constantly scrutinise food labels to check the nutritional content?
- Do you avoid certain foods even though you want to eat them?
- Do you feel stressed or guilty if your normal diet or exercise routine are interrupted?
- Do you often decline invitations to meals and social occasions involving food in case you might have to eat something 'fattening'?

weight by strict dieting (although not as extreme as anorexics) and excessive exercise. Bingeing and purging are common, although the size of a binge may not be great – certainly less than with bulimia. It's just that the sufferer perceives the amount of food to be excessive and feels guilty after eating.

What causes female athletes to develop disordered eating and eating disorders?

There is no single cause of disordered eating in athletes but, typically, it stems from a belief that a lower body weight enhances athletic success. The athlete begins to diet and, for reasons not completely understood, then adopts more restrictive and unhealthy eating behaviour. The pressures or demands of certain sports or training programmes, or the requests made by coaches to lose weight may trigger an eating disorder in susceptible individuals.

We will now look at some of the reasons behind disordered eating and eating disorders.

The demands of the sport

In competitive sport, there is a great deal of pressure on athletes to manipulate their diets in order to achieve or maintain optimum performance. It's easy to fall into the trap of thinking that weight loss is the key to improved performance.

A 1994 study at the Norwegian University of Sport found that athletes in 'thin-build' sports, who were under pressure to lose weight and conform to a certain body size and shape, were more likely to develop eating disorders and disordered eating. Those who had previously dieted or whose weight fluctuated frequently were most at risk. Other specific trigger factors included a sudden increase in training volume and stressful or traumatic events (such as injury, illness, moving away from friends and family, or change or loss of a coach). These events can leave some athletes feeling vulnerable and out of control. Attempting to lose weight then becomes their way of regaining control.

Pressure from the coach or teammates to lose weight

Sometimes a negative comment about the athlete's weight from the coach can trigger disordered eating. Several studies have found that athletes start dieting stringently after a coach advises them to lose weight but does not give them any guidance on proper weight loss. Equally, comments or teasing from teammates may trigger disordered eating in athletes, particularly in adolescents, who are more vulnerable to the negative opinions of their peers and eager to feel accepted by them.

Social and media pressures

Like many women, athletes also experience social, media and cultural pressures to be thin. In today's culture, women are constantly bombarded with messages to be thin and conform to a certain shape. It seems as if society values weight more than other characteristics. Thinness is perceived to symbolise success, self-control and happiness. The fact that so much in the sporting world is about image, with many top athletes used to promote relevant merchandise, can only serve to increase the pressure on athletes lower down the ladder to conform to some perceived ideal.

Family pressures

Female athletes may face additional pressures from their family or have a troubled home life, all of which may make them more susceptible to the disorder. A 2006 study carried out at Stanford Medical Centre, California, USA, with 455 female university students found that those who received negative comments about their weight, shape and eating from their family were more likely to develop disordered eating or eating disorders.

Typically, the family of an anorexic place excessive emphasis on physical appearance and high achievements. There is more likely to be:

- poor communication between family members
- an incapacity to resolve conflicts
- overprotective or controlling parents
- exaggeratedly high parental expectations
- unwillingness to confront new situations
- a family history of depression or alcoholism.

A study carried out in 2000 by researchers at the University of Alabama, USA, found that women with eating disorders were more likely to have parents who were critical and controlling. Family members often get involved with their child's sporting activity, attending training sessions and competitions, which often results in the young athlete 'assuming' the role of 'being the one to blame' for the family's problems.

The athlete's personality

Most women who participate in competitive sports have greater drive and more self-discipline than their peers who don't commit to practising and improving in sports. Some athletes develop compulsive food and exercise rituals as a form of self-discipline. The problem is that the very things that make someone a good athlete – discipline, competitiveness, perfectionism – also contribute to disordered eating and eating disorders.

Both athletes and non-athletes with eating disorders and disordered eating share similar personality traits: high need for approval, conformity and high personal expectations, and measure their self-worth and success by external standards (see the box on this page, on the eating disorders 'personality'). Yet, despite their accomplishments, they have low self-esteem. This becomes tied to their body weight – something they are never satisfied with but are forever trying to change. The desire to control their body weight becomes an overwhelming obsession. Researchers at the University of Leeds found that those athletes with an eating disorder had lower self-esteem and poorer psychological health than those who didn't have an eating disorder.

THE EATING DISORDERS 'PERSONALITY'

- Low self-esteem
- Perfectionism
- Tenacity or obsessiveness
- High need for approval
- High achieving
- Competitiveness

Other causes

There may also be a genetic link. Around 10 per cent of anorexics have siblings similarly affected, and it occurs more commonly than would be expected in identical twins. Researchers have identified certain genes that influence personality traits such as perfectionism and thus predispose an individual to eating disorders. Scientists have recently proposed that sufferers have a defective gene that results in abnormally high levels of the brain chemical, serotonin. This causes a reduction in appetite, lowered mood, and anxiety. They suggest that anorexics use starvation as a means of escaping anxiety.

Evidence is also emerging that people with eating disorders have disturbed body chemistry as well as a psychological predisposition to disordered eating. For example, studies have found that more than half of those suffering from anorexia have a severe zinc deficiency, and that recovery is more successful if zinc supplements are given.

Are athletes at greater risk of disordered eating than non-athletes?

Athletes are thought to be at greater risk of disordered eating than non-athletes because of their characteristic personality traits. As previously mentioned, athletes tend to be highly driven, perfectionist, self-motivated, competitive and goal-orientated – traits that are important for athletic success. But these are also the same traits seen in people with eating disorders. It's possible that the female athlete's personality may put her at greater risk than a non-athlete for developing disordered eating. Training then becomes a way to lose weight, and the positive relationship between leanness and performance further legitimises the athlete's pursuit of thinness.

Distance runners are at risk of developing disordered eating because of the close link between low body weight and performance. Those participating in aesthetic sports, such as dancing, bodybuilding and gymnastics, are at risk because success depends on body shape as well as physical skill. Athletes competing in weight division sports, such as judo and lightweight rowing, are also more susceptible to developing eating disorders due to the pressures of meeting the weight criteria.

Eating problems can develop at any time in an athlete's career, but young athletes who are approaching adolescence are most vulnerable. As their body composition and body shape changes, some girls find that their performance drops and they can no longer compete at the same level. They may feel powerless to hold back the changes associated with puberty and prevent weight gain, so begin to restrict their food intake in a misguided attempt to regain control.

Look out for the following warning signs and types of behaviour that could indicate an eating problem in athletes:

- unexplained losses in performance
- an obsession with body image, shape and weight
- constant use of weighing scales
- missing meals or avoiding certain foods
- an obsession with quantities or proportions of food in the diet
- rapid mood swings
- rapid and significant weight loss.

Are women with eating disorders attracted to certain sports?

It is possible that some people with a predisposition to eating disorders are attracted to certain sports because they provide them with a setting in which they can hide or justify abnormal eating and dieting behaviour. Endurance sports and sports that require large amounts of aerobic exercise may attract people with disordered eating because they can use exercise to burn extra calories and keep their body weight low. Since low weight and body fat is typical of these sports, it makes it difficult to identify those athletes with disordered eating.

The training programmes of certain sports may attract women who would normally use excessive exercise as a means of losing weight or controlling weight. The positive relationship between leanness and performance in sports such as distance running, gymnastics, figure skating and dancing legitimises the athlete's pursuit of thinness, so that the sport provides an ideal camouflage for an athlete's eating disorder, serving as a socially acceptable excuse to family and friends.

It's easy for athletes with eating disorders to use their sport or training as an excuse for dieting. For example, they may cut out high-fat foods or eliminate sugary foods. While this may be perfectly healthy for most athletes, anorexics can take this to an extreme and 'get away' with eating very little. Many anorexics and bulimics use excessive exercise to get thin. Clearly, this is quite different from the commitment required from dedicated athletes, but it can be difficult to distinguish between 'normal' training and obsessional exercise. Even when ill or injured, an athlete with anorexia would continue training, fearful of gaining weight. This is clearly dangerous.

Athletes with bulimia may not eat very much before a workout or competition, fearing it will make them feel 'heavy' and slow them down. Or they might not eat after exercise or competition for fear that their eating will get out of control or they will need to find a way to secretly purge. Thus a bulimic athlete may go all day without food; however, by the evening, she is likely to be very hungry, her restraint low and the temptation to binge high.

The motivating factors for restricting food intake differ between athletes and non-athletes. Non-athletes want to lose weight, whereas athletes with eating disorders want to improve their performance as well as lose weight – they believe that losing weight will help them perform better, that they have to be 'thin to win'. This is one reason why eating disorders are more common in sports that emphasise leanness.

Athletes with eating disorders tend to tie self-esteem and self-worth to athletic performance. They believe that having a low body weight is essential to achieving good performance. For bulimics, if their training or performance doesn't go as well as they want, this may knock their self-esteem and so they turn to food for comfort, thus triggering a binge-and-purge episode. Similarly, if they perform well, they reward themselves with food, which may lead to a binge. Or they may use bingeing and purging as a coping mechanism when under pressure.

Many bulimic athletes worry about eating with the team, partly in case their eating becomes out of control, and partly for fear of being discovered in a purge and confronted about their eating disorder. For them, travelling and team meals can be stressful, which provokes further anxiety and likelihood of bingeing/purging – their only coping mechanism.

Athletes with bulimia are more likely to use exercise as way of purging themselves of food than vomiting or laxatives. Since they already exercise or play sport, this makes it relatively easy for the bulimic athlete to disguise and explain away their eating disorder.

Can disordered eating affect an athlete's performance?

Ironically, in the short term, there may be an improvement, rather than a drop, in performance. Athletes with disordered eating, particularly anorexics, seem to have endless energy and feel that they can't keep still. This is the body's way of encouraging them to find food, but the signal is often misunderstood and they become more active. This may be due partly to a rise in levels of the 'fight or flight' hormones cortisol, adrenaline and noradrenaline, produced by starvation, and partly due to the psychological boost they get from losing weight. Their weight loss motivates them to train hard because they believe 'being lighter means faster'. Their personality – strong willed, highly driven and with a strong desire to succeed – means that they are often able to motivate and push themselves to exercise, despite feelings of exhaustion.

To overcome physical fatigue, many athletes with disordered eating use stimulants such as caffeine or diet pills to suppress their appetite and maintain their energy. Thus, in the short term they are able to continue training hard and performing well, in spite of their low calorie intake.

But there is a line beyond which further weight reductions will impair the body's ability to perform. Eventually, restrictive eating rebounds on health, the body will start to break down and performance will suffer. As glycogen and nutrient stores become chronically depleted, the athlete's health will suffer and optimal performance cannot be sustained indefinitely. Low glycogen stores result in increased fatigue and reduced performance. Maximal oxygen consumption decreases, cardiac output (the amount of blood that the heart pumps out) decreases, and chronic fatigue sets in. A 1991 study at the Norwegian University of Sport and Physical Education measured a drop in oxygen uptake and running speed in elite endurance runners after two months of severe dieting.

Without enough protein to maintain and repair muscle, there will be a loss of lean body mass, strength and endurance. The athlete quickly becomes more susceptible to injury, illness and infection. If fat intake is too low (less than 10 per cent of calories) the lack of fat-soluble vitamins and essential fatty acids will result in fatigue and poor performance. Deficiencies in vitamins and minerals will eventually develop, and these will affect performance too, increasing the risk of muscle weakness, injuries and infections.

Athletes who use diuretics or laxatives, or self-induce vomiting, will become dehydrated. This quickly results in fatigue and poor performance. It can also have serious effects on health. The reduced blood volume results in decreased blood flow to the skin, which means the body is not able to sweat properly and maintain a normal temperature during exercise. This, in turn, increases core temperature, and increases the risk of heat exhaustion and heatstroke.

In summary, athletes with disordered eating and eating disorders are likely to suffer from nutritional deficiencies, chronic fatigue, dehydration and a dramatic reduction in performance.

What are the health consequences of disordered eating and eating disorders?

As well as affecting performance, disordered eating and eating disorders can also have serious health and psychological consequences. Severe and sustained weight loss can lead to medical problems and to death – 20 per cent of anorexics die.

Severe food restriction and dramatic weight loss, particularly when combined with intense exercise, lead to disturbances in the menstrual cycle, abnormal oestrogen metabolism and menstrual dysfunction. Menstrual periods can become irregular (oligomenorrhoea) or stop altogether (a condition called amenorrhoea). In fact, menstrual dysfunction is relatively common among female athletes, particularly those who restrict their food intake. Scientists believe this is a result of a low energy intake combined with high energy expenditure, and is a way of conserving energy in the body in order to protect more important biological and reproductive processes. It is more common in dieting athletes with a low body weight or body fat level. Not having periods may seem very convenient to athletes, but it's a very important warning sign that all is not well.

When self-starvation becomes so severe that you stop having periods, you also produce less oestrogen. Without enough oestrogen to maintain and increase bone mass, the bones get weaker, more porous and lighter. This may result in osteopenia (a lower-than-normal bone density) or osteoporosis (more severe loss of bone density). Studies show that bone density in the spine may be 20 per cent lower in amenorrhoeic athletes compared with normally menstruating athletes. Weakened bones fracture more easily from the stresses and impacts of sports such as gymnastics and the pounding that runners absorb. Stress fractures are more common among amenorrhoeic female athletes.

Fortunately, amenorrhoea is reversible. Once an athlete begins eating properly, and body weight and body fat are restored to normal levels, her periods start again. Studies at the University of Washington have shown that, unfortunately, bone density cannot be fully restored even when athletes start eating normally and periods resume. This means that athletes with a history of amenorrhoea will always have bone densities below normal, and will be at increased risk of stress fractures and premature osteoporosis.

Hypotension (low blood pressure) and cardiac arrhythmia (heartbeat irregularities) are common, while more serious complications, such as heart muscle atrophy (wasting) and liver and kidney failure, can develop. Anorexics often suffer gastrointestinal symptoms such as pain, bloating, constipation and discomfort following eating. As the disorder advances, the body's digestive system eventually loses the ability to process food properly, and can shut down altogether – the person starves to death. As mentioned above, it has been estimated that around 20 per cent of anorexics die from their illness.

HEALTH PROBLEMS OF EATING DISORDERS

Some of the health problems suffered by women with eating disorders include:

- amenorrhoea (cessation of periods) and infertility
- heart problems, such as abnormal heart rhythm, low blood pressure and cardiac failure
- osteoporosis, weakened bones, risk of fracture
- erosion of dental enamel
- gastrointestinal problems such as peptic ulcers
- kidney problems
- low white blood cell count and poor immunity
- metabolic problems
- difficulty maintaining body temperature
- dry, scaly, itchy skin
- fine layer of hair on body.

What are the health consequences of bingeing and purging?

Regular purging gets food out of the body before it can be absorbed. This inevitably results in inadequate intake of energy and nutrients. Sufferers are likely to suffer persistent tiredness as well as symptoms of vitamin and mineral deficiencies, such as skin and gum problems.

Dental problems are common in bulimics who vomit, due to the action of stomach acid, resulting in acid erosion of the tooth enamel, cavities, and swollen and tender gums. Frequent vomiting or laxative abuse can lead to stomach pains, abdominal cramps, indigestion, constipation, diarrhoea and, in extreme cases, ulceration and perforation of the oesophagus. Purging can also result in dehydration and electrolyte imbalances, hypotension, light-headedness and poor circulation.

Fortunately, many of the health problems of bulimia, apart from enamel erosion, can eventually be reversed with treatment and a healthy nutritional programme.

How should I approach someone suspected of having an eating disorder or disordered eating?

Approaching someone you suspect of having an eating disorder or disordered eating requires great care and sensitivity. This is best done by someone with whom she has a close and trusting relationship. This may be a friend, a coach or school counsellor. Athletes with disordered eating or eating disorders are likely to deny having a problem. They may feel embarrassed and their self-esteem may be threatened. Most fear that by admitting their problem they will get kicked off the team or prevented from training. They may be embarrassed because they think eating disorders are personality flaws, or that they are the only one with an eating disorder. So it is vital to avoid direct confrontation about their eating behaviour or physical symptoms.

If you're worried that a friend may have disordered eating or an eating disorder, here are some ways you can help.

- Plan the conversation for a quiet time and place. You should make sure that you have privacy so that your friend won't feel trapped.
- Think about what you will say in advance. The purpose of your talk is to offer help.
- Ask the person how she feels, and let her know that you genuinely care. Be tactful, tread very carefully and avoid accusations. It may take several conversations over a period of time until she feels able to admit to having a problem or begins to talk about it.
- Do not present 'evidence' or confront her with accusations, such as 'You've lost too much weight.' Do not try to 'catch her out' to prove your case. This will make her more defensive and threatened, and will ultimately drive her further away from you.
- Don't make demands such as 'Stop doing this to yourself.' Eating disorders are illnesses that require proper treatment.
- Don't bargain: 'If you don't stop, I won't be your friend.' Just state your concern and your wish for your friend to seek help.
- Focus on the consequences of her eating behaviour rather than the eating behaviour itself. For example, express concern about her performance, her low mood, fatigue or frequent illnesses, rather than focus on her food intake or weight (e.g. 'I've noticed that you've been very tired lately and I'm concerned about you').
- Don't try to cure her behaviour or give solutions – for example, 'Try to eat more' – the problem is more complex than that, and your friend needs proper help from an expert.
- Do have details of an eating disorders hotline number, website, brochure or book with you (*see* the Resources section on page 128). When the conversation ends, offer to leave the details with your friend.

What should I do if the sufferer refuses to admit to a problem?

If the sufferer initially denies she has a problem (and this is most likely to be the case), leave the subject for a short while – say, two or three weeks – before approaching it again. Don't push too hard to start with. Repeated attempts may well be necessary, but avoid undue coercion. However, if she continues to deny the problem or refuse help, and there is serious concern for her health, a slightly more direct approach may be necessary. For example, ask her how much weight she has lost and then give tactful information about a healthy weight for her sport. You may try asking about her menstrual cycle, whether she feels tired and fatigued, depressed or irritable. Once she admits to any of these problems, carefully ask her about her eating habits and let her know you are concerned. Only as a last resort, and where there is great concern about her health, should you insist on a consultation with a specialist.

What should I do if the sufferer admits she has a problem?

Getting the sufferer to admit to having an eating problem is a significant accomplishment. Sometimes, the sufferer may be relieved that they will no longer have to hide their disorder. But they may refuse treatment, fearing that they will lose control or that their performance may suffer. You should be prepared to arrange treatment. Suggest to her that it would be best to have a consultation with an eating disorders specialist. Help her make arrangements for a consultation as soon as possible, before she changes her mind.

Various forms of specialist help are available, including trained counsellors from a self-help organisation or a private eating disorders clinic. A GP can provide a referral for treatment with a multidisciplinary team of psychologists and dietitians. This may be within a hospital or clinic. Bear in mind, though, that even when eating disorders are identified, treatment can take many months or years. Doctors, therapists, and supportive friends, family members and teammates can help athletes learn new ways of thinking and feeling about how they eat, why they train and what it means to be healthy.

What can I do to help myself?

Recognising you have an eating problem and wanting to get help is a big step forward, so it's important to find someone who you can trust to talk this over with – this may be a friend, or a therapist or counsellor. Phone the Eating Disorders Association helpline (*see* the Resources section on page 128). Alternatively, you can see your GP, who will offer you treatment through regular appointments or refer you to a specialist.

Seek help quickly. The longer you leave the problem, the longer you will remain trapped and isolated. You will find that your performance starts to suffer. The earlier you seek help, the sooner you can begin on the road to recovery. Recovering from an eating disorder can take time and may be a painful process. However, it is possible to gain new confidence and begin to realise that there are other ways of coping.

What type of treatment can the sufferer expect?

Different types of treatment are available, depending on the type and severity of the disorder, and also on the sufferer herself. Bulimia is usually treated on an outpatient basis, whereas anorexia can involve a period of in-patient treatment as well.

The ultimate goal of treatment is to normalise weight and eating behaviour, and to deal with the psychological issues that lie behind the eating disorder. The treatment for an anorexic involves restoring normal weight and health, as well as solving the problems that led to the development of the disorder. If you've been fasting, you'll need to start by eating small portions of easily digested food until your system learns to cope. Admission to a hospital or specialist clinic will help your recovery if you're very weak. The typical weight gain goal is no more than 0.9 kg (2 lb) per week. The treatment for a bulimic patient involves breaking the binge–purge cycle and developing a normal eating pattern.

Other options include talking treatments and self-help groups where you can talk to others with the same problem. Dance and movement therapies can also help a person to feel more connected to and happier with their body. Whatever form of help the athlete chooses, the support of friends and family is very important.

Individual therapy

Sufferers may receive individual psychotherapy with a therapist who will determine the exact nature of the eating problem and develop an individual treatment strategy. For anorexics, psychological changes often take a number of years, and require a great deal of honesty, trust and sincerity. It may take many months before an anorexic patient will start to accept treatment, gain weight and eat more. Although eating behaviours are often discussed, the surrounding emotional issues are the main focus of therapy sessions.

For bulimics, therapy usually lasts about 20 sessions over a number of months. The first stage, which lasts about a month, involves establishing control over eating.

BREAKING THE CYCLE

This guide is not intended as treatment for an eating disorder. Treatment should always be sought from an eating disorders specialist.

- Learn to accept and like your body's shape - emphasise your good points.
- Realise that losing weight will not solve deep-rooted problems or an emotional crisis.
- Don't set rigid eating rules for yourself, feeling guilty when you break them.
- Don't ban any foods or feel guilty about eating anything.
- Establish a sensible healthy eating pattern rather than a strict diet.
- Listen to your natural appetite cues - learn to eat when you are hungry.
- If you overeat, don't try to 'pay for it' later by starving yourself.
- Enjoy your exercise routine or sport; have fun instead of enduring torture to lose weight.

The second stage, lasting about two months, involves changing the patient's attitude towards food, eating behaviour and their body shape, as well as increasing their self-esteem. After this stage, a maintenance plan is drawn up.

Group therapy

A sufferer may decide to join a self-help or support group, which will provide help from a therapist but also allow her to discuss her problem with and obtain support from fellow sufferers. The goal of group treatment is to help a sufferer identify her feelings, needs, wishes and goals.

Family therapy

Sometimes family therapy is offered, particularly for younger anorexic patients. All the family members are involved in the treatment. Here, the aim is to explore family relationships, dynamics and issues that may have contributed to the development of the disorder. A family-based strategy is developed to overcome the problem. This may be done in conjunction with in-patient behavioural therapy. Here, access to pleasurable activities or possessions is granted upon weight gain.

Nutritional therapy

The sufferer may be referred to a nutritionist or dietitian for nutritional counselling at some point in her treatment. Although the sufferer believes herself to be knowledgeable about food and eating behaviour, she may actually have many misconceptions. The nutritionist or dietitian will be able to provide correct information and work out a nutritional programme suited to the individual. She will provide reassurance to the sufferer about weight gain, encourage the recovering patient to eat in a variety of different settings, and can also counsel other members of the family about nutrition. Many sufferers will have lost the ability to recognise hunger and satiety: anorexics have learned to ignore hunger; bulimics have learned to override satiety. The therapist will help the sufferer re-establish the sense of hunger and food, often with the aid of a food log where the sufferer records her food intake. This can help her understand the factors behind her eating behaviour and develop a strategy for dealing with them.

Is it possible to prevent disordered eating and eating disorders in athletes?

You need a diet that allows you to strike a balance between maintaining a particular body weight and safeguarding your health. It should supply enough calories to support your training, as well as a healthy balance of protein, fat, carbohydrate, vitamins and minerals (*see* Chapter 1). The following tips will help you achieve that balance.

- Always remember that nutrition is fundamental to good performance.
- Remind yourself that food is fuel, not just something that determines your body size.
- Your body will take from your muscles to produce energy if you have too low a calorie intake – this will reduce your muscle strength. Not something that will help your performance!
- Meals don't need to be big, but balanced.
- If you feel pressurised to lose weight, speak to your coach and seek advice from a registered nutritionist or dietitian (to find one, *see* the Resources section on page 128).
- Get as much information about sports nutrition as you can; read Chapter 1 of this book and *see* the Resources section on page 128.
- Don't cut out food groups (e.g. wheat, dairy) or impose strict food rules (e.g. no fat, no 'junk' food) – you need to choose a wide variety of different foods to get your daily quota of nutrients. Overly strict rules can sometimes result in obsessive eating behaviour.
- Avoid low-carbohydrate diets and high-protein diets as they don't provide enough energy to support a training programme.
- If you have to make a weight category for your sport, you should plan your weight loss strategy with your coach and a sports nutritionist or dietitian. Aim to lose no more than 1 kg (2 lb) per week.

Key points

- Eating disorders are a key component of the female athlete triad, a term that describes the three interrelated health conditions: low calorie intake (with or without eating disorders), amenorrhoea and bone loss.
- Those competing in 'thin-build' sports (i.e. where a low body weight, body fat

level or thin physique is perceived to be advantageous) are more prone to developing eating disorders.

- Up to 60 per cent of athletes have disordered eating patterns.
- Anorexia nervosa is an extremely restrictive eating behaviour in which the individual continues to restrict food and feel fat in spite of being 15 per cent or more below an ideal body weight.
- Bulimia nervosa refers to a cycle of food restriction followed by bingeing and purging.
- Disordered eating is a general term used to describe a wide range of abnormal and harmful eating behaviours that sufferers use to try to lose weight or maintain an abnormally low body weight.
- The pressures or demands of certain sports or training programmes, or the requests made by coaches to lose weight may trigger an eating disorder in susceptible individuals.
- Athletes may be at a greater risk of disordered eating than non-athletes because of their characteristic personality traits: highly driven, perfectionist, self-motivated, competitive and goal-orientated.
- Some women with a predisposition to eating disorders may be attracted to certain sports because they provide them with a setting in which they can hide or justify abnormal eating and dieting behaviour.
- Disordered eating and eating disorders can have serious health and psychological consequences: nutritional deficiencies, chronic fatigue, dehydration, a dramatic reduction in performance, menstrual dysfunction, osteopenia, osteoporosis and stress fractures.
- Various forms of specialist help are available, including trained counsellors from a self-help organisation or a private eating disorders clinic.
- The ultimate goal of treatment is to normalise weight and eating behaviour, and to deal with the psychological issues that lie behind the eating disorder.

03

BODY COMPOSITION AND SPORTS PERFORMANCE

Many female athletes desire a lean physique. This tends to be driven by performance as competitive standards get higher as well as a desire to achieve a socially acceptable weight and shape. For most sports, a low body fat percentage means better performance, while a high body fat percentage can reduce speed, agility and efficiency of movement.

This chapter examines the issue of optimal body composition for sport and how body fat levels may affect your performance. It outlines a healthy weight loss strategy that will allow you to continue to train hard without losing energy.

How can I measure my body fat percentage?

There are many methods of assessing a person's fat and lean mass. The most common methods include those described below.

Underwater weighing

Underwater weighing has been considered the 'gold standard' for body composition assessment. It is based on Archimedes' principle of displacement, which states that:

- the density of fat mass and fat-free mass are constant
- lean tissue is more dense than water
- fat tissue is less dense than water
- therefore a person with more body fat will weigh less underwater and be more buoyant.

With this method you are weighed while submerged in a large tank of water. This value is then compared with your weight on dry land, using computer software. However, this method is not generally accessible to the public and new, more sophisticated methods may make underwater weighing obsolete in the future.

Skinfold thickness measurements

Because underwater weighing is expensive and requires special equipment, many coaches and exercise trainers use simple skinfold measurements to determine body fat percentage. The American College of Sports Medicine says that, when performed by a trained, skilled, tester, this method is up to 98 per cent accurate.

With this method, skinfold callipers are used to measure the amount of subcutaneous fat at specific sites on the body: typically mid-biceps, mid-triceps, subscapular (below the shoulder blade), supra-iliac (above the hip bone), lower back, and sometimes the abdomen and mid-thigh. The tester pinches the skin at the appropriate site to raise a double layer of skin and the underlying adipose tissue, but not the muscle. The callipers are then applied 1 cm below and at right angles to the pinch, and a reading in millimetres taken two seconds later. The mean of two measurements should be taken.

Because of the increased likelihood of error with this method, many physiologists use the sum of several sites to monitor and compare body fat measures.

Alternatively, you may convert the measurements into body fat percentages using various standard equations – for example, the Yuhasz equation (Yuhasz, 1974) for females:

% body fat = (0.1548 × sum of triceps, subscapular, supraspinae, abdominal, thigh, calf) + 3.58

Table 3.1 gives general guidelines for using the total sum (in millimetres) of the main skinfold sites (triceps, subscapular, supraspinae, abdominal, thigh, calf).

Table 3.1 Guidelines for using total sum (mm) of main skinfold sites

		Excellent	Good	Average	Below average	Poor
Normal	Male	60–80	81–90	91–110	111–150	150+
	Female	70–90	91–100	101–120	121–150	150+
Athletic	Male	40–60	61–80	81–100	101–130	130+
	Female	50–70	71–85	86–110	111–130	130+

Sometimes, exercise physiologists prefer to record skinfold thickness measurements along with body girth measurements (i.e. chest, waist, hips, upper arm, thigh and calf). This allows you to monitor changes in body fat distribution.

Bioelectrical impedance

Body composition and body fat analysers and scales available for home use are based on the principle of bioelectrical impedance. These devices determine total weight, the percentage and amount of body fat, muscle mass, water and even bone mass. While the readings can be affected by hydration levels, skin temperature and other factors, if you follow the directions and always take the reading under similar conditions, you will obtain fairly accurate results.

In this method, a mild electrical current passes through the body, either from foot to foot or foot to opposite hand. It relies on the principle that lean tissue is a good

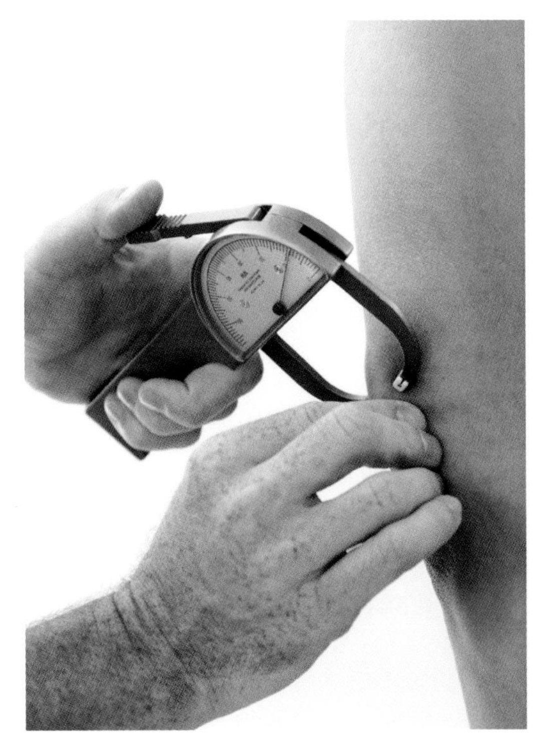

conductor of electricity, while body fat creates a higher resistance. In other words, the current moves much more easily and more quickly through lean mass, but much more slowly through fat mass. Thus the amount of current flowing through the body reflects the relative amount of body fat: the more body fat you have, the greater the resistance.

However, this method is less accurate for very lean and very fat people.

Dual energy X-ray absorptiometry (DEXA)

A DEXA scan is the most accurate method for measuring body fat. It is painless and you are not enclosed by the equipment at any stage during the scanning process. The scanner itself consists of a large, flat table, which you lie on during the scan. Beneath the table is an X-ray generator. The DEXA machine sends a thin, invisible beam of very low-dose X-rays from two different sources through the body. The amount of X-rays that come through the tissue from each of the two X-ray sources is measured by a detector. The ratios can then be used to predict total body fat, fat-free mass and total body bone mineral. The denser the tissue is, the fewer X-rays get through to the detector. This information is sent to a computer, which generates an image of the body. The procedure can take about 10–20 minutes.

Unfortunately, due to their cost and size, DEXA machines are not generally accessible to the public. They are used mostly for measuring bone density to diagnose osteoporosis, but are also used in hospital and university research departments for body composition analysis – some offer a body composition analysis for sportspeople.

What is my ideal body fat percentage?

According to scientists at the University of Arizona, the ideal body fat percentage for most elite female athletes lies between 12 and 18 per cent. A typical 60 kg elite female athlete with 15 per cent body fat would, therefore, have about 9 kg of body fat. This is, of course, considerably lower than the average body fat level of healthy non-athletic women: about 18–30 per cent.

However, the ideal body composition does not exist, nor is there a linear relationship between body fat percentage and performance. For each person, there is an optimal fat percentage at which she will perform at her best. For this reason, sports physiologists believe that a range of values for body fat percentage should be established, outside of which your performance and/or health is likely to be impaired. Staying below the upper limit should be your target, but lower is not necessarily better. Typical ranges for female athletes are shown in Table 3.2. The lowest body fat levels are observed in female bodybuilders, distance runners, cyclists and triathletes.

Table 3.2 Body fat percentages in various sports

Sport	Male	Female	Sport	Male	Female
Baseball	12–15%	12–18%	Skiing (X-country)	7–12%	16–22%
Basketball	6–12%	20–27%	Sprinters	8–10%	12–20%
Bodybuilding	5–8%	10–15%	Swimming	9–12%	14–24%
Cycling	5–15%	15–20%	Tennis	12–16%	16–24%
Gymnastics	5–12%	10–16%	Triathlon	5–12%	10–15%
High/long jumpers	7–12%	10–18%	Volleyball	11–14%	16–25%
Ice/field hockey	8–15%	12–18%	Weightlifters	9–16%	No data
Racquetball	8–13%	15–22%	Wrestlers	5–16%	No data
Rowing	6–14%	12–18%			
Shot putters	16–20%	20–28%			

What is the minimum amount of body fat I need?

A certain amount of body fat is vital for the body to function normally and healthily. In fact, striving for a body fat percentage that is too low can be dangerous.

Your total body fat percentage can be divided into two categories, as follows.

1. *Essential body fat:* for the body to function normally and healthily, a certain amount of body fat is required. This is called essential fat and includes the fat that forms part of your cell membranes, brain tissue, nerve sheaths, bone marrow, and the fat surrounding vital organs, where it provides cushioning and protection. For both men and women, this amounts to about 3 per cent of body weight. However, women also store fat in the breasts and around the hips, and this accounts for a further 5–9 per cent of body weight. Thus, for women, the average amount of essential fat is 8–12 per cent of body weight, and for men it is 3 per cent.
2. *Storage fat:* this consists mainly of fat deposited just under the skin (subcutaneous fat) and fat in the abdominal cavity (intra-abdominal fat). Some storage fat is required for good health. It is used to provide energy for day-to-day activities, as well as for sports and exercise. Although not all of this is available as fuel, the amount of storage fat is much greater than that needed for immediate energy

production. Even in an event as long as a marathon, only about 200 g of body fat is needed for energy.

Obviously the amount of storage fat varies between individuals, and between men and women. An excess of storage fat, however, serves no useful function for athletes.

How does body composition affect performance?

Excess body fat hinders sport performance. This is true of all activities in which the body weight must be moved through space, such as running and jumping. That's because excessive body fat tends to reduce speed, agility, balance and endurance, and increase fatigue. It slows you down and reduces your mechanical efficiency. In weight division sports, such as karate and judo, the person with the lowest percentage of body fat and highest percentage of lean mass will have the performance advantage. Even in sports where a large body weight is important for generating momentum, such as discus and hammer throwing, the athlete with the highest percentage of lean mass performs better. Perhaps the only sport where extra fat is considered advantageous is sumo wrestling. It is almost impossible to attain a very high body weight without fat gain.

In general, then, low body fat levels are associated with better performance. But the relationship between body fat percentage and performance is not necessarily a linear one. Being lean will not guarantee you athletic success. It is likely that lean athletes are lean because they do more training. And the harder you train, the better you perform. Obviously the more training you do, the leaner you are likely to be. A study with runners carried out at Aberdeen University in the UK showed that the runners who covered the greatest distance in training had the lowest body fat levels. Interestingly, they also ate more food than those who did less running.

Isn't extra fat advantageous for swimming?

Extra body fat may appear to give swimmers an advantage. In one sense it does: it increases their buoyancy so less effort is required to stay afloat and move through the water. Certainly with younger swimmers, those carrying more body fat appear to have a performance advantage. But after puberty, as the body shape changes, the buoyancy advantage of extra fat diminishes.

Extra fat now starts to reduce your swimming speed. It increases 'friction drag' around the more protruding areas of the body (e.g. abdomen and buttocks). It also increases frontal surface resistance in the water. Thus, a swimmer with higher body fat must expend more energy than a lean swimmer over any given distance. In competitive swimming, those swimmers who have the leanest and the most streamlined physiques are able to swim fastest.

Body fat: how low is too low?

Reducing your body fat may lead to improvements in performance, but if the loss is too rapid or too severe, then your performance and health may suffer.

Trying to achieve a body fat percentage that is so low it affects your essential fat stores is *not* good for your health. So women should not let their body fat levels go below about 10–15 per cent. This isn't a target level, rather a minimum level below which your health and performance will suffer. Attaining extremely low levels of body fat invariably involves chronic under-eating. Nutrient deficiencies and fluid/electrolyte imbalance from low food intake can lead to impaired immunity, increased risk of infection and illness, loss of reproductive function, and serious medical conditions such as dehydration and starvation.

For female athletes, low body fat levels cause a drop in oestrogen levels. This in turn can lead to a loss of bone mass and increased risk of fracture. The female athlete triad highlights the problem. This refers to the presence of three conditions often found in female athletes who lose too much body fat: eating disorders, amenorrhoea and decreased bone mass (*see* Chapter 2, page 41). The medical complications of this triad involve almost every body function, and include the cardiovascular, endocrine, reproductive, skeletal, gastrointestinal, renal and central nervous systems.

What are the risks of low body fat levels?

Although there is a strong link between body fat levels and exercise performance, it's important to recognise that reducing body fat levels will not automatically guarantee success, and may even be counterproductive. If you cut your food intake too drastically not only will your training suffer, but the risk of illness and injury increases too.

Amenorrhoea tends to be triggered once body fat levels fall below 15–20 per cent, although the threshold varies from one person to another. This fall in body fat, together with other factors, such as low calorie intake and heavy training, is sensed by the part of the brain called the hypothalamus, which then decreases its production of the hormone (gonadotrophin-releasing hormone) that acts on the pituitary gland. This, in turn, reduces the production of important hormones that act on the ovaries (luteinising hormone and follicle-stimulating hormone), causing them to produce less oestrogen and progesterone. The end result is a deficiency of oestrogen and progesterone, and a cessation of menstrual periods.

Low body fat levels also upset the metabolism of the sex hormones, reducing their potency and thus fertility. Therefore, a very low body fat level drastically reduces a woman's chances of getting pregnant. However, the good news is that, once your body fat level increases over your threshold and your training volume is reduced, your hormonal balance, periods and fertility generally return to normal.

Amenorrhoea can result in a loss of bone minerals and a reduction in bone density. In younger (pre-menopausal) women, this is called osteopenia (i.e. lower bone density than normal for age), which is similar to the osteoporosis that affects post-menopausal women, where bones become thinner, lighter and more fragile. Amenorrhoeic athletes, therefore, run a greater risk of stress fractures.

What is a healthy way to reduce body fat?

To lose body fat, you have to expend more energy than you consume. Research has shown that a combination of diet and activity is more likely to result in long-term success than diet or exercise alone. Avoid any weight loss methods that promise quick results – you are unlikely to get enough calories or carbohydrate to support intense training, and you may end up losing lean tissue as well as fat. Low-carbohydrate diets will leave you with depleted muscle glycogen stores, which results in lethargy and poor performance. Unfortunately, there are no miracle solutions or short cuts.

For healthy weight loss, the American College of Sports Medicine recommends that athletes reduce their calorie intake by approximately 10–20 per cent. This modest calorie drop should produce a weight loss in the region of 0.5 kg per week, and avoid the metabolic slowdown that is associated with more severe calorie reductions. You can achieve this by cutting fat and, only if necessary, carbohydrate intake by around 10–20 per cent. Reducing your carbohydrate intake further may result in a loss of strength and endurance. Aim to get 20–25 per cent of total calories from fat, and 1.2–1.7 g protein per kg of body weight daily.

How can I calculate my calorie, carbohydrate, protein and fat requirements?

To help guide you, the following calculations are for a female athlete weighing 60 kg and 168 cm (5 feet 6 inches) tall.

Step 1: Estimate your basal metabolic rate (BMR) (*see* pages 7–8, Chapter 1)

BMR = 665 + (9.6 × W) + (1.8 × H) – (4.7 × Age) = daily calorie needs
Where:
W = weight in kg
H = height in cm
Age = years

665 + (9.6 × 60) + (1.8 × 168) – (4.7 × 30)
665 + 576 + 302 – 141 = **1402** kcal per day

Step 2: Multiply your BMR by your PAL (*see* Table 1.1, page 8)

Daily calorie needs = BMR × PAL. So, for the daily energy needs for the 60 kg female athlete:

1402 × 1.5 = 2103 kcal

This is the number of calories you need to maintain your body weight.

Step 3: Reduce your calorie intake by 15 per cent

To do this, multiply your maintenance calories, as calculated in step 2, by 0.85 (85 per cent) to give you your new total daily calorie intake. Example:

New total daily calorie intake = 2103 × 85 per cent = 1788 kcal

Step 4: Calculate your carbohydrate needs

In a 24-hour period, during low- or moderate-intensity training days, you should get 5–7 g carbohydrate per kg of body weight. During moderate to heavy endurance training, 7–10 g per kg is recommended. However, as your calorie needs decrease by 15 per cent, so should your usual carbohydrate intake. So, for the 60 kg female athlete doing low–moderate training:

Maintenance carbohydrate intake = (60 × 5) - (60 × 7) = 300 - 420 g
Carbohydrate intake for weight loss = (85% × 300 g) - (85% × 420 g) = 255 - 357 g

Step 5: Calculate your protein needs

Endurance athletes require between 1.2 and 1.4 g protein per kg of body weight per day. That's 72–84 g daily for a 60 kg woman. Strength athletes require 1.4–1.7 g per kg of body weight per day, or 84–102 g daily.

Step 6: Calculate your fat needs

You should aim to achieve a fat intake between 20 and 25 per cent of your calorie intake. So, for a female athlete consuming 1788 calories daily:

$(1788 \times 20\%)/9 = 40$ g
$(1788 \times 33\%)/9 = 50$ g
i.e. between 40 and 50 g fat a day.

> **IS IT POSSIBLE TO SPEED UP FAT LOSS?**
>
> Increasing your exercise calorie expenditure will help speed up fat loss. This can have a dual effect. First, any additional aerobic exercise you perform on top of your regular training will increase fat oxidation during exercise. Second, adding or increasing weight training exercises will offset any loss of lean tissue and maintain muscle mass.

What's the best strategy for healthy weight loss in female athletes?

Step 1: Set yourself a goal

Goals help focus your mind and keep you on track. Not having a goal means allowing circumstance or other people to determine your fate. You have to believe in and truly want to achieve your goal. The first step is to assess where you are now and where you want to be. Then write it down in as much detail as possible. A good goal (sometimes referred to as a SMART goal) is made up of the following five elements:

1. *Specific:* it's easier to plan for and achieve a specific goal than a vague one. Clearly define what you want to achieve (e.g. 'I want to achieve a body fat percentage of 20 per cent.').
2. *Measurable:* you need to be able to measure your progress, otherwise you won't know whether you have reached your goal (e.g. measure body fat percentage or body weight or chest/waist/hips/arm/leg circumferences).
3. *Agreed:* commit your goal to paper – you will be much more likely to achieve it than if you simply kept it as a thought in your head. Writing down your goal signals a commitment to change and makes it more likely that you will achieve your goal.

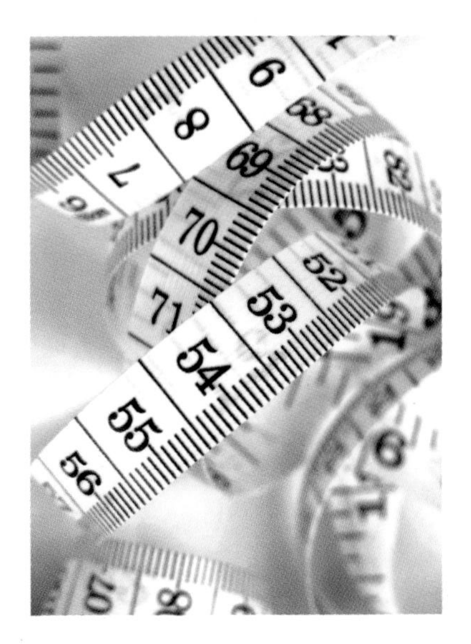

4. *Realistic:* your goal has to be realistic and attainable for your body shape and lifestyle (e.g. 'I will lose 3 kg in six weeks').
5. *Timescaled:* set a clear and realistic timescale. Break your goal into smaller mini-goals and set specific daily tasks.

Step 2: Monitor body composition changes

The best way to ensure you are losing fat not muscle is to measure your body composition once a month. Use one of the methods of body composition measurement described on pages 65–67.

Step 3: Aim to lose no more than 0.5 kg per week

Weekly or fortnightly weighing can be useful for checking the speed of weight/fat loss, but do not rely exclusively on this method as it does not reflect changes in body composition. Avoid more frequent weighing as this can lead to an obsession with weight. Bear in mind that weight loss in the first week may be as much as 2 kg, but this is mostly glycogen and its accompanying fluid.

HOW TO REDUCE SATURATED FAT

Substitute:

- semi-skimmed or skimmed milk instead of full-fat milk
- chicken, fish and lean meat instead of processed meat, burgers, meat pies, pâté and sausages
- fresh fruit instead of desserts, chocolate and cakes
- fresh or dried fruit and nuts instead of high-fat snacks when you're on the go.

Cook low fat:

- use small amounts of unsaturated oils such as sunflower, olive and rapeseed, instead of butter, lard and ghee
- boiling, steaming, grilling and stir-frying are healthier ways to cook your food
- eat chicken and turkey without the skin
- trim the fat off meat, and try grilling meat instead of frying.

Flavour without fat:

- top baked potatoes with fromage frais, yoghurt, a little pesto or baked beans
- have salads with low-fat salad dressings, balsamic or flavoured vinegars, and low-fat yoghurt seasoned with fresh herbs, lemon or lime juice, rather than mayonnaise and oily dressings
- add flavour with fat-free condiments such as mustard, herbs, herb salt, soy sauce and salsa.

Compare labels:

- when you're shopping, compare similar foods and choose the option that is lower in saturated fat
- 'high' is more than 5 g saturated fat per 100 g; 'low' is 1.5 g saturated fat per 100 g.

Step 4: Keep a food diary

A food diary is a written record of your daily food and drink intake. It is a very good way to evaluate your eating habits, and to find out exactly what, why and when you are eating. It will allow you to check whether your diet is well balanced or lacking in any important nutrients, and to take a more careful look at your usual meal patterns and lifestyle.

Weigh and write down everything you eat and drink. Be honest – every spoonful of sugar in tea, every scrape of butter on bread should be recorded.

Use your food diary to find out about the main sources of saturated fat and sugar in your diet, and then work out which foods you can eliminate or cut back on.

Step 5: Reduce saturated and hydrogenated fats

Look carefully at your current eating habits and focus on cutting saturated rather than unsaturated fats. The box titled 'How to reduce saturated fat' provides suggestions.

Step 6: Eat mostly foods with a low energy density

The most filling foods are those with a high volume per calorie, or a 'low energy density'. If you can eat a plate of food that is low in calories relative to its volume, you're likely to feel just as satisfied as eating smaller amounts of high-calorie food. High-fibre foods with a high water content, such as fruit, vegetables, pulses and wholegrain foods, give maximum fill for minimum calories. Their high fibre content slows down the emptying of food from your stomach, making you feel full for longer. Fibre also gives food more texture, so you need to chew your food more. Energy density is the number of calories per gram. To work out a food's energy density, simply divide the number of calories in 100g by 100. Try to select mostly foods with an energy density less than 1.5, and eat smaller portions of foods with higher energy densities (see Table 3.3).

Step 7: Don't ban your favourite foods

Including your favourite foods in moderation will make your fat-loss plan easier to stick to, if not pleasurable. Studies have shown that when people are allowed to indulge in their favourite food in moderation, they are more likely to adhere to their weight loss plan. If you know that you can eat a little of your favourite food every day, you'll stop thinking of it as a forbidden food and then won't want to binge on it. So go ahead and include chocolate or ice cream in your nutrition plan, but make sure it's only a little.

Table 3.3 The energy density of foods

Very low energy density 0–0.6 Eat satisfying portions	Most fruits (e.g. strawberries, apples, oranges), non-starchy vegetables (e.g. carrots, broccoli), salad vegetables (e.g. lettuce, cucumber), skimmed milk, clear soups, fat-free or plain yoghurt
Low energy density 0.6–1.5 Eat satisfying or moderate portions	Bananas, starchy vegetables (e.g. sweetcorn, potatoes), low-fat plain/fruit yoghurt, pulses (beans, lentils, peas), pasta, rice and other cooked grains, breakfast cereals with low-fat milk
Medium energy density 1.5–4.0 Eat moderate–small portions	Meat, poultry, cheese, eggs, pizza, chips (fries), raisins, salad dressings, bread, ice cream, cake
High energy density 4.0–9.0 Eat small portions or substitute low-fat versions	Crackers, crisps, chocolate, sweets, croissants, biscuits, cereal bars, nuts, butter and oils

Are popular diets healthy and effective?

Most diets work in the short term, but not all are healthy and most are not sustainable in the long term. The more extreme the diet, the lower the chance of adhering to it. A year-long study at the Tufts New England Medical Center in the USA compared four different diets (Atkins diet, Ornish low-fat diet, WeightWatchers and the Zone diet) and found that all produced a similar, albeit small, weight loss (three-quarters of participants lost less than 5 per cent of their body weight in a year), but that few dieters could stick to them for long enough to make a permanent difference. They found that most dieters reduced their calorie intake initially, but levels crept back up again. Of the diets tested, the low-carb Atkins diet achieved the lowest weight loss over 12 months and had the lowest adherence.

A 2006 UK study compared the effectiveness and nutritional content of four commercial slimming programmes: SlimFast, Atkins, WeightWatchers and Rosemary Conley's Eat Yourself Slim diet. The researchers found that all the diets result in a reduced calorie intake, resulting in an average weight loss after eight weeks of between 3.7 kg and 5.2 kg. There was no significant difference in weight loss between the diets themselves. On the whole, the diets provided the RDAs for most nutrients, but dieters failed to increase significantly their consumption of fruit and vegetables as recommended.

The secret to losing weight is to eat more healthily, increase your activity and make step-wise changes to your lifestyle that you are comfortable with and will be able to adopt long term. Failing to keep to a diet can not only affect your health and metabolism but can cause psychological problems. A two-year study at the University of California in 2005 found that overweight women who did not follow a set diet but simply ate more healthily and listened to hunger and satiety cues, improved their health (e.g. blood pressure and cholesterol levels) and had higher self-esteem. In contrast, those who dieted for six months regained their weight and reported significant drops in confidence and self-esteem.

Healthy weight loss checklist

- Set yourself a realistic weight or body fat goal that is right for your body type.
- Keep a food diary – this helps you become aware of your true eating pattern.
- Do not skip meals or starve yourself during the day.
- Plan three meals and one or two healthy snacks throughout the day.
- Remember, there are no banned foods – all foods are allowed.
- Do not set yourself rigid eating and exercising rules. Be flexible and never feel guilty if you overindulge or miss an exercise session.
- Examine your feelings and emotions when you eat. Food should not be used as a shield for emotional problems. Solve these with the help of a trained counsellor or eating disorder specialist.

Key points

- The most common methods for measuring body composition include underwater weighing, skinfold thickness measurements, bioelectrical impedance and dual energy X-ray absorptiometry.
- For each person there is an optimal fat percentage at which she will perform at her best – for most elite female athletes, this lies between 12 and 18 per cent.
- A certain amount of body fat is vital for the body to function normally and healthily.
- Excess body fat adds to the weight that has to be carried, and thus increases the energy cost of exercising. Reducing this will lead to improvements in performance but if the loss is too rapid or too severe, your performance and health may suffer.
- Severe reductions in body fat can result in low oestrogen levels, loss of bone mass and increased risk of fracture.
- To lose body fat, you have to expend more energy than you consume – a combination of diet and activity is more likely to result in long-term success than diet or exercise alone.
- For healthy weight loss, the American College of Sports Medicine recommends that athletes reduce their calorie intake by approximately 10–20 per cent.

AMENORRHOEA AND SPORT

Many female athletes experience irregular menstrual cycles, but some stop having regular periods altogether (amenorrhoea). While you may view this as a desirable side-effect of training as they no longer have to deal with the inconvenience and discomfort of monthly periods, it is in fact a serious health condition that can result in irreversible bone loss, a higher risk of stress fractures and long-term problems with osteoporosis starting from an early age. Amenorrhoea can also markedly reduce the chances of conception should you want to start a family.

What is amenorrhoea?

Amenorrhoea is a term used to describe the absence for more than three months of menstrual cycles (defined by the American College of Sports Medicine's Position Stand on the Female Athlete Triad, 2007). In athletes it is sometimes called exercise-associated amenorrhoea and is one of the three interrelated components of the female athlete triad (*see* page 41, Chapter 2).

There, in fact, are two types of amenorrhoea:

1. primary amenorrhoea, where periods have never started (delayed menarche)
2. secondary amenorrhoea, where periods stop after menarche.

How common is amenorrhoea in female athletes?

The number of female athletes with amenorrhoea varies considerably with sport, age, training volume and body weight. Amenorrhoea is certainly more common in 'thin-build' sports' (*see* page 43), in particular ballet (between 24 and 79 per cent) and long-distance running (24–65 per cent). Studies have also found that approximately 12 per cent of swimmers and 12 per cent of cyclists are affected.

What causes amenorrhoea?

There's no single cause of amenorrhoea, but you are more likely to develop the condition if you:

- have lost weight quickly
- have a low body weight
- have a low percentage of body fat
- exercise very hard
- had irregular periods before you started training
- follow a restrictive diet
- feel emotionally stressed.

Whatever the combination of risk factors, amenorrhoea results from a disruption to the normal production of hormones that control the menstrual cycle. In a normal cycle, a small area of the brain called the hypothalamus produces gonadotrophin-releasing hormone (GRH) in regular 'pulses' through the day. GRH then acts on the pituitary gland (just below the brain) to release other hormones – luteinising hormone (LH) and follicle-stimulating hormone (FSH) – also in 'pulses' through the day. These, in turn, release oestrogen and progesterone from the ovaries, which trigger menstruation.

Amenorrhoea develops when, for various reasons, the normal production of GRH is disrupted. This has an immediate knock-on effect, reducing the production of FSH, LH, oestrogen and progesterone. The ovaries stop ovulating and menstrual periods stop.

The following factors are likely to contribute to amenorrhoea in athletes:

A low body fat level

Low body weight and body fat levels are often linked with amenorrhoea, but these aren't necessarily the cause of the condition. Many female athletes with 'normal' body fat levels experience amenorrhoea; conversely, many female athletes with very low body fat levels do not have amenorrhoea. In other words, there isn't any evidence for a 'critical level' of body fat to maintain a normal menstrual cycle.

The latest thinking is that a rapid loss of body fat together with a low body fat percentage can trigger amenorrhoea. In other words, it is the speed of weight loss rather than having a low body fat level per se that can determine whether you develop amenorrhoea.

Too much exercise

There is mounting evidence that prolonged intense endurance exercise can cause a fall in GRH levels, which, in turn, leads to amenorrhoea. This is why many experts now term the syndrome 'exercise-associated amenorrhoea'.

One study of female runners showed an almost linear relationship between weekly mileage and the prevalence of amenorrhoea. Approximately 28 per cent of those running 40 miles a week had amenorrhoea; 45 per cent of those running 80 miles a week were affected. By contrast, only 2 per cent of age-matched sedentary women had amenorrhoea.

It's not known whether it is the volume or intensity of training that causes the hormonal disruptions, but normal menstrual cycles can be regained by reducing or cutting training volume (e.g. reducing the weekly mileage) as well as reducing training intensity.

A low calorie intake

Many female athletes restrict their food consumption in the misguided belief that they are too fat or that losing weight will improve their performance. One study found that amenorrhoeic runners consumed an average of 300 fewer calories than runners who had normal menstrual cycles.

But many athletes may be in 'negative energy balance' even if they are not consciously restricting their food intake at all; they simply do not eat enough food to fuel their exercise energy expenditure. A busy lifestyle, travel, stress and other factors can result in an inadequate calorie intake.

Scientists now believe that a chronically low energy intake combined with high energy expenditure (intense exercise) is responsible for triggering the hormonal changes that result in menstrual irregularities. It doesn't matter if the imbalance is due to an intentional caloric restriction or an increase in exercise. Your periods stopping is a warning sign that the body is under too much stress and has too little energy stored to support healthy functioning.

The body needs to be in 'energy balance' for normal hormonal and menstrual functioning. When there is an imbalance (i.e. energy intake is less than energy output) over a period of time, then the normal production of GRH is disrupted. Experts speculate that a woman stops ovulating and menstruating to protect against pregnancy during extreme physiological stress. Amenorrhoea may be a way of conserving energy in the body in order to protect more important physiological processes.

An eating disorder

In some athletes, amenorrhoea and chronic dieting may be forerunners of an incipient eating disorder. It is one of the symptoms, or diagnostic criteria, of anorexia nervosa, which is common in sports where a low body weight and body fat are desirable (*see* page 43). The American Psychiatric Association's definition of anorexia lists 'absence of at least three consecutive menstrual cycles' among its criteria. Other criteria include weight loss 15 per cent below that expected, intense fear of gaining weight or becoming fat, and distorted body image. A study of 50 elite distance runners at the British Olympic Medical Centre found that 50 per cent of the amenorrhoeic athletes had sub-clinical or clinical eating disorders. By contrast, only 12 per cent of normally menstruating women had eating disorders.

Previous menstrual irregularities

Women who started their periods late or who have had previous menstrual irregularities are more likely to develop amenorrhoea when they start to train intensively. Conversely, women are less likely to develop amenorrhoea when they train after having children. Even athletes who have had prolonged amenorrhoea prior to pregnancy often have regular periods afterwards. This is probably due to an increase in body weight and body fat.

Too much stress

It is well recognised that women can stop having periods during times of stress. Often, the pressures of training, competition and a busy lifestyle combine, and this physical and emotional stress can trigger changes in the body's hormonal output. This can disrupt the menstrual cycle and result in irregular or absent periods. When the stress is reduced, then normal menstrual cycles can resume.

What are the health risks of amenorrhoea?

Long-term menstrual irregularities and amenorrhoea can cause serious health problems. The biggest risk is a loss of minerals from the bones. With this comes almost a three times higher incidence of stress fractures and early osteoporosis. A total of 24 per cent of athletes with no or irregular periods experience stress fractures, compared with 9 per cent of regularly menstruating athletes.

Without enough oestrogen to maintain bone mass, the bones get weaker, more porous and lighter. This may result in **osteopenia**, a lower than normal bone density, or **osteoporosis,** more severe loss of bone density. Studies show that bone density in the lower spine may be 20–30 per cent lower in amenorrhoeic athletes compared with normally menstruating athletes. Weakened bones fracture more easily from the stresses and impacts of sports such as gymnastics, and the pounding that runners absorb.

The lack of oestrogen not only causes a loss of minerals but also slows the rate of bone turnover. This means that the rate of new bone formation is less than that of bone loss. Micro-fractures occur more easily and heal more slowly. The full bone

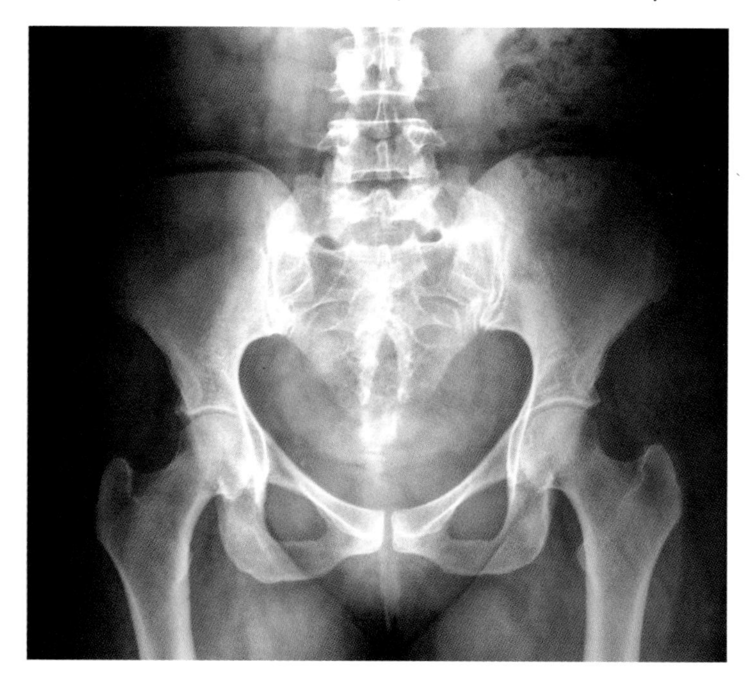

turnover cycle takes about three months, and major changes in training volume or intensity should therefore be planned over this period of time. If training is increased too rapidly, microscopic fractures can occur in the bone. If these are not allowed to heal (due to training) they can lead to a stress fracture.

Normally, weight-bearing exercise has a positive effect on bone density, but in amenorrhoeic athletes, bone density falls and may even be lower than that of non-active women. For example, runners would normally have a higher bone density in the hips, but those with amenorrhoea have considerable bone loss despite intense training. Training cannot compensate for the negative effects of low oestrogen levels. Studies have shown a linear relationship between the number of periods per year and bone density – the fewer the periods the lower the bone density.

Restricting your calorie intake results in high levels of cortisol – the 'stress' hormone – which can also cause a loss of bone minerals. Canadian researchers have correlated menstrual irregularities with high cortisol levels.

Is there long-term damage?

When you resume your normal menstrual cycle, you can restore some but not all of your bone density. That's why amenorrhoea should sound an alarm that all is not well. It is important you take steps to treat amenorrhoea and resume periods as soon as possible. However, amenorrhoea may persist for and take up to six months to reverse.

Are there other health risks of amenorrhoea?

If you have amenorrhoea then you are infertile due to the cessation of ovulation and normal menstrual function. Thus, amenorrhoea can markedly reduce the chances of conception should you want to start a family.

Oestrogen also has an effect on ligaments and tendons. Studies on runners and dancers have found a higher frequency of soft tissue injuries in those with menstrual irregularities. It is unclear why this occurs, but it may be related to low levels of oestrogen. For instance, during pregnancy, when oestrogen levels are high, the mother's ligaments become more supple and stretch more easily. This enables the pelvis to widen during birth. It is possible that the opposite applies in athletes: when oestrogen levels are very low, the ligaments become less supple and more susceptible to injury.

How can amenorrhoea be treated?

Since the underlying problem with exercise-related amenorrhoea is a mismatch between energy intake and expenditure, coupled with a high level of physical stress caused by a high training volume, the key to treating the condition is to increase food intake and reduce training volume.

Experts advise lowering the intensity and volume of your training by 10–15 per cent and eating a little more. You may also need to adjust your training programme to include short periods of lower-intensity training and more rest.

Studies show that when amenorrhoeic athletes improve their diet and restructure their training programme to improve energy balance, normal menstruation resumes within about three months and performance improves consistently.

The following tips may help you resume normal menstrual cycles:

- If you have suffered amenorrhoea for longer than six months, seek advice from your GP to rule out medical causes of amenorrhoea.
- Be realistic about your goal weight – you may be striving to attain a weight lower than that appropriate for your genetic body type.
- If you have weight to lose, don't crash-diet but rather cut back on calories by about 15 per cent. Seek advice from a nutritionist or dietitian if you are struggling to balance food intake and exercise.
- Aim to lose weight/body fat gradually, while minimising loss of lean mass.
- Eat at least 20 per cent of your calories from fat. It won't make you fat: some fat is crucial for health and sports performance. Eat mainly unsaturated fats found in oily fish, nuts, avocado, and olive and other plant oils.
- Ensure you consume adequate calcium to maintain bone density. Include three or four servings of dairy products or other calcium-rich foods daily (*see* page 35).
- Reduce your training frequency, volume and intensity, or change your current programme to include more cross-training.
- If you have some degree of disordered eating, you will need help in overcoming this problem (*see* page 49).

Do I need to gain body weight in order to resume normal menstrual cycles?

Even small increases in body weight may be all that is necessary to resume menstrual cycles. Studies are ongoing to determine just how many calories are needed for normal menses to resume, but, so far, it appears that even small increases in body weight (1–3 kg) may be all that is required to resume normal menstrual cycles, by reversing the negative energy balance that caused the problem.

Do I need to see my doctor for amenorrhoea?

If amenorrhoea persists after making the above changes, you should see your doctor. They may do various tests to find out why you stopped menstruating. They may advise reducing your training intensity and volume, and increasing your overall calorie intake. Sometimes they advise increasing your calcium intake as well. If regular periods don't begin again within six months of making changes in exercise and diet, your doctor may consider prescribing hormone therapy to prevent further loss of bone mineral density. Doses of oestrogen and progesterone, similar to those used for treating post-menopausal women, are usually used. Supplements containing calcium, magnesium and other key minerals may be advised simultaneously.

How can amenorrhoea be prevented?

The best way to prevent amenorrhoea is by learning to recognise the warning signs and taking steps to prevent it.

- Monitor your menstrual cycle by using a diary or calendar.
- Consult your doctor if you have menstrual irregularities, have recurrent injuries or stress fractures.
- Seek counselling if you suspect you are overly concerned about your body image – for example, if you are constantly striving to be thin.
- Consult a sports nutritionist to help you design an appropriate diet that is specific to your sport and to your body's energy needs.
- Seek emotional support from family, friends, coaches and teammates.

Key points

- Amenorrhoea is the absence of menstrual cycles lasting more than three months, and is one of the three interrelated components of the female athlete triad.
- Amenorrhoea is more common in 'thin-build' sports'.
- There's no single cause of amenorrhoea – but you are more likely to develop amenorrhoea if you have lost weight quickly, have a low body weight, have a low percentage of body fat, exercise very hard, had irregular periods before you started training, have a restrictive diet or feel emotionally stressed.
- It is thought that a chronically low energy intake combined with high energy expenditure (intense exercise) is responsible for triggering menstrual irregularities.
- Amenorrhoea is a warning sign that the body is under too much stress and has too little energy stored to support healthy functioning.
- Health problems associated with amenorrhoea include irreversible bone loss and osteoporosis.
- The condition may be treated by increasing food intake and reducing training intensity/volume by 10–15 per cent.

05

NUTRITION AND EXERCISE IN PREGNANCY

Female athletes share the same nutritional recommendations for pregnancy as non-athletes but there are additional issues. These relate to weight gain and body composition, which tend to differ markedly from non-athletic women. Many female athletes – particularly those in sports requiring a very lean physique, such as endurance events, aesthetic sports and weight division sports – tend to have a lower body fat percentage than non-athletic women. In addition, the physical and psychological demands of regular exercise may affect your chances of conception and of a successful pregnancy. This section highlights the sports-specific issues associated with pregnancy.

Will low body fat levels affect my ability to get pregnant?

Your chances of conception depend on whether your menstrual cycle is normal. If you are having periods every 28 days or so, it's likely that your weight and body fat aren't interfering with ovulation and won't affect your chances of getting pregnant.

But, if you have very low body fat levels, then this may make it more difficult to conceive. A study at Greenville Hospital, South Carolina, USA, found that underweight women were about half as likely to get pregnant as normal-weight women.

When body fat is too low, it disrupts the flow of hormones from the brain to the pituitary gland. This means that the normal signal from the pituitary gland to tell your ovaries to release an egg doesn't happen. So, even if you have plenty of healthy eggs, you won't be able to get pregnant because you're not releasing them.

As explained in Chapter 4, amenorrhoea and loss of normal menstrual function is not simply a result of a very low body fat. A combination of factors is normally involved, including a chronic low calorie intake, high training volume and intensity, and emotional and physical stress. Many female athletes are affected by one or more of these factors and, thus, fertility can be low and the chances of pregnancy small.

If you are not having regular periods, your doctor will probably suggest that you ease up on your training a bit and take in more calories to increase your body fat. Even small increases in body weight may be all that is necessary to resume menstrual cycles. Normal menstrual function and fertility can usually be restored within six months by adjusting your training programme to include short periods of lower-intensity training and more rest, and increasing your calorie intake by 10–15 per cent.

How much weight should I gain during pregnancy?

The ideal amount of weight you should put on depends on your pre-pregnancy weight. On average, a healthy weight gain is 10–12.5 kg (22–28 lb) over 40 weeks. Although there are no specific recommendations for weight gain during pregnancy in the UK, the American College of Obstetricians and Gynaecologists encourages thinner women to gain a little more weight: around 12.8–18 kg (28–40 lb).

The majority of the weight will be spread fairly evenly over the last two trimesters, about 0.5 kg (1 lb) per week, with a little more at the end. About one-quarter of your weight gain (3–4 kg/6–9 lb) will be the weight of your baby; about half (6 kg/13 lb) will be pregnancy-related weight (placenta, amniotic fluid, uterus, extra blood, breast tissue); and about one-quarter (3–4 kg/6–9 lb) will be extra body fat. Table 5.1 lists where the weight goes.

Table 5.1 Body composition changes during pregnancy

Baby	3.4 kg
Placenta	0.65 kg
Amniotic fluid	0.8 kg
Uterus	0.97 kg
Breast tissue	0.41 kg
Blood	1.25 kg
Water	1.68 kg
Fat	3.35 kg
Total	**12.5 kg**

Most of the extra fat gain occurs in the second trimester, mostly around the upper thighs, hips and abdomen under the influence of progesterone. This extra fat deposit acts as a buffer of energy for late pregnancy when the developing baby's energy needs are highest.

During late pregnancy and post-pregnancy, the body produces the hormone lactogen to mobilise these fat stores to provide energy for the developing baby and breast milk production should your calorie intake drop. In practice, this extra fat is not necessary as there is little danger of a drop in food supply. Most women have already got enough body fat to buffer against a food shortage.

What are the dangers of gaining too much weight in pregnancy?

Being overweight and gaining too much body fat can increase your blood pressure. It can also increase your risk of complications such as gestational diabetes and pre-eclampsia. Gestational diabetes can lead to the birth of a larger than normal baby, while pre-eclampsia is characterised by dangerously high blood pressure and can progress to a more serious seizure-inducing condition. Very overweight women are more likely to have extra-large babies, which may need forceps or Caesarean delivery. You are also at increased risk of infections such as those of the urinary tract.

Will having low body fat cause any problems during pregnancy?

Provided you are in good health and are gaining weight at the recommended rate, a low body fat level should not present a problem. Many women who are naturally very slim go on to have healthy babies. However, if you are gaining very little weight you should seek the advice of your midwife or doctor.

What are the dangers of gaining too little weight?

Gaining too little weight during pregnancy is not recommended as this may have an adverse effect on your baby. The baby is more likely to be underweight when born, shorter in length and have a smaller head circumference than normal. If you are underweight at the start of pregnancy, make sure you gain at least 12.5 kg.

How many calories should I eat during pregnancy?

During the first two trimesters of pregnancy, the extra amount of food energy required is very small indeed. So, contrary to popular belief, you don't need to eat for two. The Department of Health (DoH) recommends no change in calorie intake. During the third trimester, there is a greater increase in your energy needs as the baby grows larger and additional pregnancy-related tissues are laid down. The DoH recommends an extra 200 kcal daily during this time. But this is not a hard-and-fast rule as it depends on your pre-pregnancy weight and how active you are through the pregnancy. In general, overweight women may need fewer extra calories, while underweight women may need more.

However, as an athlete, you may not need to eat more food because the discomfort of the growing bump may curtail your normal physical activity level. If you reduce your training substantially, you may need to adjust your food intake to match your activity level. It is fine to continue exercising during pregnancy, but you will almost certainly need to reduce the intensity and/or frequency of your training during the third trimester (due to your increased weight and the physiological changes associated with pregnancy).

Is it dangerous to restrict calories during pregnancy?

Many athletes, who have trained hard to maintain a lean physique, find it difficult to accept increases in their body weight during pregnancy, and may be tempted to restrict their fat gain by restricting calorie intake. Those already prone to disordered eating are particularly vulnerable. But dieting or calorie restraint during pregnancy is potentially harmful to the health of both the developing baby and the mother.

Eating too few calories over a period of time may restrict the baby's growth and development, and result in a low birth weight. Skipping meals and leaving prolonged gaps between eating leads to a fall in blood sugar levels, which will not only make you feel light-headed and lethargic, but may also affect the baby's development. However, the developing foetus is surprisingly resilient and, even if the mother's nutritional intake is low, the foetus takes what it needs from the mother's stores. In this way, nature aims to protect the foetus at the expense of the mother.

Vitamin, mineral and calcium needs

During pregnancy, there is an increased need for most vitamins, particularly during the last trimester. The DoH advises a modest increase in your intake of thiamine, riboflavin, folate, and vitamins A, C and D. This should be achievable from a balanced diet but, as precaution against deficiency, you may wish to take a multivitamin and mineral supplement.

The DoH recommends taking a daily folic acid supplement containing 400 µg (micrograms) (0.4 mg) prior to pregnancy and during the first 12 weeks to reduce the risk of neural tube defects, such as spina bifida. The RDA for folate is 200 micrograms; Table 5.2 gives the folate content of various foods.

Table 5.2 The folate content of various foods

Food	Folic acid (micrograms (µg)/portion)
100 g broccoli	64
Large (200 g) baked potato	88
100 g Brussels sprouts	110
100 g cabbage	29
100 g spinach	90
1 orange	50
40 g bran flakes	100
4 g yeast extract	40
150 g chickpeas	81

Do I need extra minerals?

There are no official recommendations to increase your dietary intake of minerals during pregnancy – the developing baby takes what it needs from your stores and also your body absorbs a greater percentage of these minerals from the food you eat. For example, the absorption of iron increases from about 7–10 per cent to 30–40 per cent during the last trimester in order to meet the increased needs. Nevertheless, it is advisable to include plenty of iron-rich foods in your diet (*see* Table 5.3) and to safeguard against depleted iron stores. The RDA for iron is 14.8 mg, but you should not take supplements unless you have been diagnosed as iron-deficient and advised to do so by your doctor.

Table 5.3 The iron content of various foods

Food	Iron content (milligrams/portion)
140 g steak	2.9
130 g chicken breast	0.8
100 g canned sardines	2.3
3 tbsp (120 g) cooked red lentils	2.9
200 g baked beans	2.8
2 eggs	1.6
2 slices wholemeal bread	1.3
100 g broccoli	1.0
100 g spinach	1.7

Do I need extra calcium during pregnancy?

Calcium is an important nutrient during pregnancy, particularly during the last 10 weeks when the baby's bones are growing fast, but the DoH does not recommend consuming extra calcium when you are pregnant. This was reaffirmed by a 2008 study carried out at the Medical Research Council in Cambridge, UK, which found no relationship between calcium intake and bone mineral content. Although the baby takes up more calcium during the last trimester as it starts to develop and strengthen its bones, the mother's increased capacity to absorb dietary calcium makes up for this loss without the need for extra intake. The recommended intake for non-pregnant women (700 mg) remains unchanged during pregnancy. An extra 500 mg a day is recommended during breast-feeding. Dairy products, canned small fish, figs and oranges are good sources of calcium.

Table 5.4 Foods containing 200 mg calcium

Almonds	83 g
Broccoli	10 sprigs (500 g)
Cheddar cheese	40 g approx.
Dried figs	4 figs (80 g)
Ice cream	2.5 scoops (250 g)
Milk	1 glass (170 ml)
Milkshake	1 glass (180 ml)
Oranges	3 oranges
Pizza	1 slice (105 g)
Sesame seeds	2 tbsp (30 g)
Tinned sardines	1.5 (36 g)
Tofu	1 slice (40 g)
Yoghurt	1 carton (130 g)

Should I limit my caffeine intake during pregnancy?

The Food Standards Agency advises pregnant women to limit their caffeine intake to 200 mg a day, equivalent to two mugs of coffee, although caffeine is also present in tea, chocolate and cola. Too much caffeine may result in a baby having a lower birth weight than it should, which can increase the risk of some health conditions later in life. High levels of caffeine may also increase the risk of miscarriage.

Table 5.5 The caffeine content of various foods and drinks

Food/drink	Caffeine (mg)
Instant coffee	100
Filter coffee	140
Tea	40–75
Cola	40
'Energy' drink	80
50 g plain chocolate	50
50 g milk chocolate	25

How much alcohol is safe during pregnancy?

Ideally, it is best to avoid alcohol completely during pregnancy. Studies show that women who drink alcohol while pregnant are more likely to give birth to babies who are smaller, premature or born with abnormalities, including foetal alcohol syndrome. For this reason, NHS adviser, the National Institute for Health and Clinical Excellence (NICE), advises pregnant women to drink no alcohol, especially in the first three months. It says that, if they must drink, they should limit their intake to one or two units a week thereafter.

Should I take an omega-3 supplement during pregnancy?

As most of the growth and development of the baby's brain and nervous system takes place before birth (and during the first two years), it is important for pregnant and breast-feeding women to consume plenty of omega-3s.

Breast-feeding is important, as breast milk supplies omega-3s for babies. Studies show that pregnant women who consume plenty of omega-3s are less likely to give birth to children who suffer from learning and behavioural problems, such as dyslexia, dyspraxia and attention deficit hyperactivity disorder (ADHD), which affects around one in 20 children. Research from Purdue University in the USA has shown that children with ADHD have lower blood concentrations of omega-3 fats.

WHAT TO AVOID

- Vitamin A supplements, fish liver oil supplements, liver and liver pâté since very high doses (more than 10 times the RDA) may lead to birth defects
- Raw or lightly cooked eggs and products made with them, because of the risk of salmonella poisoning
- Mould-ripened soft cheeses, such as Camembert and Brie, and also blue-veined cheeses, to reduce the risk of listeria poisoning
- Tuna, swordfish and marlin – these fish contain high levels of mercury, which may damage the unborn baby's nervous system.

Can I continue to exercise during pregnancy?

There's every reason to continue exercising while you are pregnant. Several studies have suggested that exercise during pregnancy will help with an easier and shorter labour and birth, reduce the risk of Caesarean delivery, lead to a quicker recovery after birth and a quicker return to your pre-pregnancy weight, not to mention feeling healthier throughout your pregnancy.

The American College of Obstetricians and Gynecologists states that, for healthy women, exercise during pregnancy is not a high-risk activity for the foetus and, if you were previously active, you may continue exercising at the same intensity as before.

SAFE SPORTS DURING PREGNANCY

- **Brisk walking** gives a good overall workout and does not put too much stress on the joints and muscles.
- **Swimming** works all the major muscles of the body. The water supports your weight, so you reduce the risk of injury and muscle and joint strain. It also helps you stay cool during exercise.
- **Cycling** is a good cardiovascular activity. However, your growing belly can affect balance and make you more prone to falls, so you may prefer to do stationary or recumbent cycling.
- **Water aerobics** and any exercise routine performed in water are safer for the joints than impact activities.

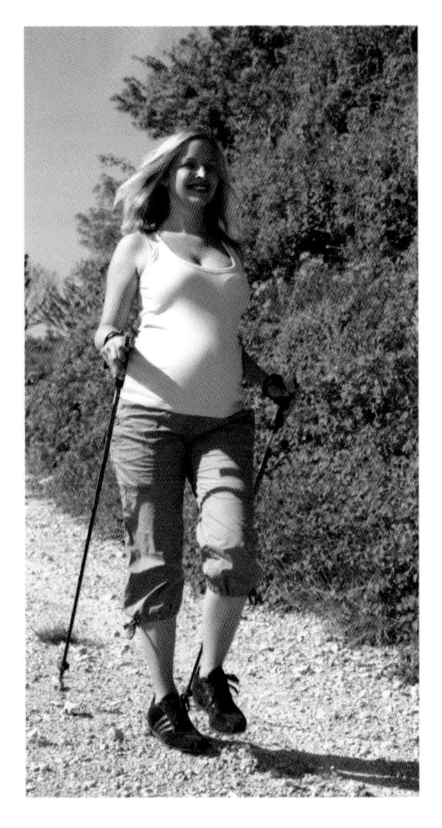

Are there any changes I need to make to my training routine?

Being pregnant may mean modifying your training a bit. Do not exercise to the point that you are exhausted. Avoid activities that involve jumping, jarring movements or quick changes in direction that may strain your joints and cause injury. Wear comfortable clothing that will help keep you cool, and a bra that fits well and gives lots of support. In addition, the British Olympic Association recommends:

- avoiding prolonged or strenuous exertion during the first trimester
- avoiding isometric exercises or straining while holding your breath
- eating a balanced diet to keep your energy levels up, and staying well hydrated
- avoiding exercising in hot, humid environments
- avoiding exercising while lying on your back, from the fourth month of pregnancy
- avoiding activities that involve physical contact or danger of falling
- wearing protective clothing
- periodic rest periods, which may help to minimise possible temperature stresses to the foetus
- knowing reasons when to stop exercise (*see* 'When must I stop exercising?', below) and consulting an obstetrician immediately if they occur.

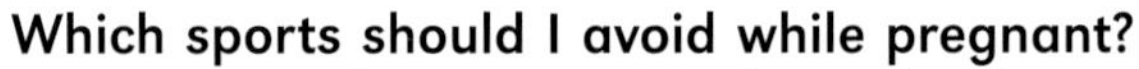

Which sports should I avoid while pregnant?

Pregnancy involves increased body weight along with hormonal preparation of the joints for birth. The ligaments that support your joints become more mobile and more susceptible to injury on impact or sudden exertion. So, avoid jerky or bouncy movements that can result in injury. The extra weight that you are carrying at the front of your body shifts your centre of gravity and places stress on the joints and on the pelvis and lower back. This can make you less stable, cause joint pain and make you more likely to lose your balance and fall, especially in late pregnancy. Activities with a higher risk of falls, such as skiing or skating, should be considered more carefully, especially after the first trimester.

The following sports should be avoided:

- downhill skiing – changing your centre of gravity can cause balance problems and put you at risk of serious injuries and falls; even if you are an experienced skier, some hazards are beyond your control
- contact sports, such as ice hockey, soccer and basketball, could result in harm to you and your baby
- scuba diving – the large amount of pressure from the water may put your baby at risk of decompression sickness
- gymnastics, water skiing and horse riding – there is an increased risk of falling.

Is it OK to run during pregnancy?

Experienced runners may be able to continue for some time, although you may have to reduce the mileage. But pregnancy is not the time to take up running or any other impact exercise.

It's a good idea to avoid running (and other high-intensity exercise) in hot, humid conditions. The extra weight you are carrying will make your body work harder than before you were pregnant. Exercise increases the flow of oxygen and blood to the exercising muscles and away from other parts of your body, so it's important not to overdo it. If your core body temperature rises beyond 39°C (102°F) there is a chance of harming the foetus. Stick to moderate exercise intensities at low to moderate temperatures.

Can I train with weights during pregnancy?

If you normally train with weights then there's no reason to stop, provided you take account of the risks discussed above – avoiding the supine position, getting too hot – and are aware of joint and balance issues. Stronger muscles can help prevent some of the aches and pains in pregnancy. But you may need to use lighter

WHEN MUST I STOP EXERCISING?

Here are 10 warning signs that you should stop exercising.

1. Vaginal bleeding
2. Breathlessness before exertion
3. Dizziness
4. Headache
5. Chest pain or heart palpitations
6. Muscle weakness
7. Calf pain or swelling
8. Pre-term labour
9. Decreased foetal movement
10. Amniotic fluid discharge.

weights (heavy weights may increase your blood pressure too much) and, during the later stages of pregnancy, consider dumbbell and body weight exercises with a fitness ball. As your centre of gravity changes, stick to seated rather than standing exercises, to avoid the risk of losing your balance.

When can I resume exercising after the birth?

Generally this will be about four to six weeks postpartum for a vaginal birth and six to eight weeks for a Caesarean birth. Ask your midwife or doctor about returning to exercise.

Key points

- Having a very low body fat level may make it more difficult to conceive.
- On average, a healthy weight gain is 10–12.5 kg (22–28 lb) over 40 weeks. Being overweight and gaining too much body fat can increase your blood pressure, and lead to the risk of gestational diabetes and pre-eclampsia.
- Gaining too little weight during pregnancy makes it more likely that your baby will

be underweight when born, be shorter in length and have a smaller head circumference than normal.

- No increase in calorie intake is recommended during the first two trimesters of pregnancy. During the third trimester, an extra 200 kcal is advised.
- Dieting or calorie restraint during pregnancy are potentially harmful to the health of both the developing baby and the mother.
- During pregnancy, there is an increased need for most vitamins, particularly during the last trimester: thiamine, riboflavin, folate, and vitamins A, C and D. A daily folic acid supplement containing 400 μg (micrograms) (0.4 mg) prior to pregnancy and during the first 12 weeks can reduce the risk of neural tube defects.
- There are no official recommendations to increase your dietary intake of minerals during pregnancy.
- Exercise during pregnancy will help with an easier and shorter labour and birth, reduce the risk of Caesarean birth, and lead to a quicker recovery after birth and a quicker return to your pre-pregnancy weight.
- Avoid prolonged or strenuous exertion during the first trimester, exercising in the supine position from the fourth month of pregnancy, and activities that involve physical contact or danger of falling, and jerky or bouncy movements that can result in injury.

MAIN DISHES

Chicken balti with sweet potato and cauliflower

SERVES 4

2 tablespoons (30 ml) olive oil
400 g chicken breast fillets, cubed
1 large sweet potato, peeled and sliced
½ cauliflower, divided into florets
500 g jar balti sauce

1. Heat the oil in a large frying pan or wok, add the chicken and stir-fry for 6–8 minutes or until pale golden.
2. Add the sweet potato and cauliflower, and stir-fry for a further 4 minutes.
3. Add the balti sauce and half a jar of water, then bring to the boil.
4. Simmer for 10–15 minutes or until the vegetables are tender.
5. Serve with pilau rice.

Nutritional analysis (per serving)

Calories	309 kcal
Protein	27 g
Carbohydrate	20 g
Total sugars*	9.0 g
Fat	13 g
Saturates	1.8 g
Fibre	3.4 g
Salt**	1.1 g

* includes sugars found naturally in foods
** excludes salt added to the recipe

Chicken with lemon and herb couscous

SERVES 4

400 g chicken breast fillets
3 tablespoons (45 ml) olive oil
1 garlic clove, crushed
2 unwaxed lemons
1 tablespoon (15 ml) fresh rosemary, chopped
1 teaspoon paprika
225 g couscous
1 red pepper, deseeded and sliced
1 yellow pepper, deseeded and sliced

1. Place the chicken breasts in a large, clean plastic food bag, seal, then beat them with a rolling pin to flatten out to about a 1 cm thickness.
2. Place 2 tablespoons of the oil, the garlic, zest and juice of the lemons, the rosemary and paprika in a shallow dish. Add the chicken and turn to coat. Cover and place in the fridge and marinate for 3-4 hours.
3. Heat a large, heavy-based frying pan until very hot. Add the chicken with the marinade and cook for 6–7 minutes on each side until thoroughly cooked. Remove from the pan and keep warm.
4. Meanwhile, cook the couscous according to the pack instructions.
5. Heat the remaining tablespoon of oil and stir-fry the peppers until just starting to soften. Remove and mix with the couscous. Serve the chicken with the couscous.

Nutritional analysis (per serving)

Calories	360 kcal
Protein	34 g
Carbohydrate	34 g
Total sugars*	4.9 g
Fat	11 g
Saturates	1.6 g
Fibre	1.3 g
Salt**	<0.1 g

Roasted sea bass with lemon and fennel

SERVES 4
2 bulbs fennel
2 tablespoons (30 ml) olive oil
2 lemons, halved horizontally
2 whole sea bass (about 1 kg in total), gutted, scaled and cleaned
Salt and freshly ground black pepper

1. Preheat the oven to 220°C (gas mark 7). Lightly oil two roasting dishes.
2. Remove the fennel tops, then cut the bulbs into thick wedges.
3. Heat 1 tablespoon of the olive oil in a heavy-based frying pan. Add the lemons, cut side down, and the fennel, and fry until golden and caramelised – about 5 minutes for the lemons, longer for the fennel wedges because you'll have to turn them.
4. Stuff the sea bass with the fennel tops, and season well inside. Put the fish in the roasting dishes and brush lightly with olive oil.
5. Arrange the caramelised lemons and fennel around the fish. Bake for 20–25 minutes or until the fish is opaque and comes away easily from the bones. Serve straight away with the lemon and fennel, accompanied by new potatoes and spinach.

Nutritional analysis (per serving)

Calories	308 kcal
Protein	49 g
Carbohydrate	1.4 g
Total sugars*	1.3 g
Fat	12 g
Saturates	1.8 g
Fibre	1.8 g
Salt**	0.5 g

Spaghetti Bolognese

SERVES 4
1 onion
2 garlic cloves, peeled
1 tablespoon (15 ml) olive oil
350 g minced turkey
3 celery stalks, chopped
2 carrots, chopped
1 tin chopped tomatoes
2 tablespoons (30 ml) tomato puree
1 teaspoon (5 ml) mixed herbs
A little low-sodium salt and freshly ground black pepper
350 g wholewheat spaghetti

1. Finely chop the onion and peeled garlic. Fry them in the olive oil over a medium heat until the onions soften, about 4 minutes. Add the minced turkey and cook, stirring for about 4–5 minutes until no longer pink.
2. Add the vegetables. Cook for a further 3–5 minutes until just tender.
3. Stir in the chopped tomatoes, tomato purée, herbs and seasoning to taste. Heat through.
4. Meanwhile, cook the spaghetti in plenty of boiling water according to the directions on the packet. Drain, then divide between four bowls and spoon over the bolognese sauce.

Nutritional analysis (per serving)

Calories	513 kcal
Protein	39 g
Carbohydrate	68 g
Total sugars*	12 g
Fat	11 g
Saturates	2.5 g
Fibre	10 g
Salt**	0.6 g

Turkey stir-fry with mango

SERVES 4
1 tablespoon sunflower oil
400 g turkey breast, cut into strips
1 large mango
1 onion, sliced
1 lime, juice of
1 tablespoon Thai fish sauce
200 g green cabbage, thinly sliced

1. Heat the oil in a wok or large non-stick frying pan. Add the turkey strips and stir-fry for 8–10 minutes until golden and there is no pink meat. Transfer to a plate, cover and keep warm.
2. Halve the mango lengthways on either side of the stone. Place the two halves flesh side up and score a lattice pattern into the flesh, without cutting through the skin. Gently push up from underneath the skin side to make the cubes stand out. Cut these away from the skin and trim any excess flesh from around the stone.
3. Reheat the pan. When hot add the onion, lime juice, fish sauce and cabbage. Stir-fry for 2 minutes. Return the turkey to the pan and stir in the mango.
4. Serve immediately with cooked basmati rice.

Nutritional analysis (per serving)

Calories	181 kcal
Protein	26 g
Carbohydrate	11 g
Total sugars*	9.3 g
Fat	3.9 g
Saturates	0.7 g
Fibre	2.7 g
Salt**	0.5 g

* includes sugars found naturally in foods
** excludes salt added to the recipe

Sweet and sour chicken

SERVES 4
2 tablespoons sunflower oil
4 chicken breast fillets, cut into 1 cm pieces
2 onions, sliced
250 g broccoli, divided into small florets
1 teaspoon grated fresh ginger

For the sweet and sour sauce:
4 tablespoons water
2 tablespoons each dry sherry, sesame oil and white wine vinegar
1 tablespoon light soy sauce
2 teaspoons honey

1. For the sauce, combine the water, sherry, sesame oil, vinegar, soy sauce and honey.
2. Heat half the sunflower oil in a wok or large frying pan, add the chicken and quickly brown on all sides for 2–3 minutes. Transfer to a warm plate.
3. Heat the remaining oil, add the onions and cook for 1–2 minutes until softened. Add the broccoli and ginger followed by the sauce.
4. Bring to the boil and then simmer gently for 3 minutes. Return the chicken to the wok and continue to cook for a further 2–3 minutes until thoroughly cooked. Serve with basmati rice.

Nutritional analysis (per serving)

Calories	315 kcal
Protein	36 g
Carbohydrate	11 g
Total sugars*	7.3 g
Fat	13 g
Saturates	2.0 g
Fibre	3.2 g
Salt**	0.2 g

Fish with spicy chickpeas

SERVES 4

1 lemon, zest and juice
3 tablespoons olive oil
4 × 140 g white fish fillets (e.g. halibut, haddock, monkfish), skinned
1 onion, sliced into thin wedges
1 red pepper, sliced
250 g packet fresh spinach, stems trimmed
½–1 teaspoon dried chilli flakes
420 g canned chickpeas, rinsed and drained
Small handful of fresh coriander, chopped

1. Preheat the grill. Mix the lemon zest with one tablespoon of the olive oil. Line a roasting tin with foil, oil lightly and add the fish. Brush the fish with the lemon oil. Season and grill for 8–10 minutes until cooked (no need to turn it).
2. Meanwhile, heat the rest of the oil and cook the onion and pepper over a moderate heat until translucent. Add the spinach and cook for a minute until wilted. Stir in the chilli flakes.
3. Tip in the chickpeas and one tablespoon of lemon juice, heat through and season. Spoon the chickpea mixture on to hot plates and serve the fish on top. Scatter over the coriander and drizzle with a little extra oil or lemon juice.

Nutritional analysis (per serving)

Calories	331 kcal
Protein	35 g
Carbohydrate	19 g
Total sugars*	5.8 g
Fat	14 g
Saturates	1.9 g
Fibre	56 g
Salt**	0.8 g

Chicken noodle salad

SERVES 4

3 tablespoons (45 ml) soy sauce
2 garlic cloves, crushed
1 tablespoon (15 ml) olive or sesame oil
300 g chicken fillets, cut into strips
350 g noodles
400 g mangetout
225 g bean sprouts
225 g carrots, grated
200 g Chinese leaves or spring greens, chopped
Lemon juice, to season

1. Combine the soy sauce, garlic cloves and oil in a bowl. Add the chicken, stir to coat and leave to marinate in the fridge for 1 hour or longer.
2. Cook the noodles according to directions on the packet. Drain.
3. In a large bowl, combine the noodles, mangetout, bean sprouts, carrots and Chinese leaves.
4. Dry-fry the chicken in a non-stick pan until cooked through. Toss in the salad and season with the lemon juice.

Nutritional analysis (per serving)

Calories	526 kcal
Protein	35 g
Carbohydrate	79 g
Total sugars*	12 g
Fat	9.8 g
Saturates	0.7 g
Fibre	7.6 g
Salt**	0.7 g

Fish and bean cassoulet

SERVES 4

750 g haddock steaks
1 litre stock or water
1 bay leaf
1 tablespoon (15 ml) oil
1 onion, chopped
2 celery sticks, chopped
2 carrots, chopped
4 tablespoons white wine or water
400 g can haricot beans, drained
1 teaspoon mixed herbs
4 tomatoes, chopped
4 tablespoons fresh breadcrumbs
2 tablespoons fresh chopped parsley

1. Cook the fish in the stock or water with the bay leaf for about 10–15 minutes. Drain, reserving 1 pint of the liquid.
2. Flake the fish, removing any bones.
3. Heat the oil in a pan and fry the vegetables for about 5 minutes.
4. Pour in the reserved fish liquid, wine or extra water, beans and herbs, and cook for about 10 minutes until the liquid has been reduced.
5. Add the cooked fish and tomatoes. Check the seasoning and transfer into a shallow baking dish.
6. Mix the breadcrumbs and parsley together and scatter over the top.
7. Bake at 190°C (gas mark 5) for 30–35 minutes until the top is crisp and golden.

Nutritional analysis (per serving)

Calories	340 kcal
Protein	43 g
Carbohydrate	33 g
Total sugars*	8.1 g
Fat	4.9 g
Saturates	<1 g
Fibre	7.0 g
Salt**	0.7 g

Chicken and vegetable curry

SERVES 4

2 tablespoons (30 ml) olive oil
1 large onion, chopped
3 skinless chicken breasts, cut into chunks
1 garlic clove, crushed
2 tablespoons medium curry paste
225 g wholegrain rice
600 ml chicken stock
230 g can chopped tomatoes
1 large carrot, sliced
75 g frozen peas
25 g toasted flaked almonds to serve

1. Heat the oil in a large, deep frying pan, and fry the onion and chicken for 5–6 minutes until the onion has softened and the chicken is browned all over
2. Then add the garlic and curry paste, and cook for 1 minute.
3. Next, stir in the rice, stock, tomatoes and carrot, and bring to the boil.
4. Cover and simmer for 15 minutes, stirring occasionally.
5. Stir in the peas, bring to the boil and cook uncovered for about 5 minutes until all the liquid has been absorbed.
6. Finally, scatter over the flaked almonds and serve with raita and naan bread, if liked.

Nutritional analysis (per serving)

Calories	448 kcal
Protein	30 g
Carbohydrate	55 g
Total sugars*	8 g
Fat	14 g
Saturates	1.8 g
Fibre	3.9 g
Salt**	0.5 g

* includes sugars found naturally in foods
** excludes salt added to the recipe

Chicken casserole with lentils and leeks

SERVES 4

2 tablespoons (30 ml) extra virgin olive oil
4 chicken breasts
2 leeks, trimmed and thickly sliced
1 onion, sliced
2 large carrots, peeled and sliced
4 sage leaves, roughly chopped
125 g puy lentils
500 ml chicken stock
A little low-sodium salt and freshly ground black pepper, to taste
2 tablespoons (30 ml) chopped fresh parsley

1. Heat the oven to 190°C (gas mark 5).
2. Heat the oil in a flameproof casserole dish on top of the stove and brown the chicken.
3. Add the leeks, onions and carrots, and continue cooking for a few minutes.
4. Add the sage, lentils and stock, and bring to the boil.
5. Season with the low-sodium salt and black pepper.
6. Cover and simmer in the oven for 1 hour or until the chicken is very tender, stirring halfway through cooking.
7. Stir in the parsley just before serving.

Nutritional analysis (per serving)

Calories	338 kcal
Protein	39 g
Carbohydrate	25 g
Total sugars*	8.8 g
Fat	9.7 g
Saturates	1.9 g
Fibre	6.1 g
Salt**	0.2 g

Pasta with chicken and mushrooms

SERVES 4

300 g wholewheat pasta
300 g skinless, boneless chicken breasts
1 tablespoon (15 ml) extra virgin olive oil
2 garlic cloves, crushed
1 tablespoon (15 ml) cider vinegar
1 tablespoon (15 ml) chopped fresh tarragon
150 g mushrooms, sliced
150 g asparagus spears
1 tablespoon (15 ml) cornflour
400 ml skimmed milk (or soya, rice or oat 'milk')
A little low-sodium salt and freshly ground black pepper

1. Cook the pasta according to the packet instructions. Drain.
2. Slice the chicken into thin strips.
3. Heat the olive oil in a heavy-based pan. Add the chicken and garlic, and cook, stirring, for 5 minutes. Add the vinegar and tarragon.
4. Stir in the mushrooms and asparagus, and cook for a further 2–3 minutes.
5. In a jug, blend the cornflour with a little of the milk to make a smooth paste. Stir in the remainder of the milk. Gradually add to the chicken mixture over a gentle heat, stirring continuously, until the sauce has thickened. Season to taste.
6. Add the sauce to the drained pasta. Mix together and serve immediately.

Nutritional analysis (per serving)

Calories	430 kcal
Protein	31 g
Carbohydrate	68 g
Total sugars*	6.2 g
Fat	5.4 g
Saturates	1.0 g
Fibre	6.7 g
Salt**	0.3 g

VEGETARIAN MAIN DISHES

Mixed bean and lentil hotpot with fresh coriander

SERVES 4

1 tablespoon (15 ml) olive or rapeseed oil
1 onion, chopped
1 garlic clove, crushed
1 red pepper, diced
125 g red lentils
500 ml vegetable stock
2 carrots, sliced
410 g tin mixed beans in water, rinsed and drained
1 tablespoon (15 ml) lemon juice
A little low-sodium salt
A small handful of fresh coriander, finely chopped

1 Heat the oil in a heavy-based pan and sauté the onions for 5 minutes. Add the garlic and red pepper, and continue cooking for 1 minute, stirring continuously.
2 Add the lentils, stock, carrots and beans. Bring to the boil. Cover and simmer for about 25 minutes, then season with the lemon juice and low-sodium salt. Finally, stir in the fresh coriander.
3 Serve with cooked quinoa or brown rice and a spoonful of low-fat natural yoghurt.

Nutritional analysis (per serving)

Calories	242 kcal
Protein	15 g
Carbohydrate	39 g
Total sugars*	9.0 g
Fat	3.9 g
Saturates	0.6 g
Fibre	8.7 g
Salt**	0.1 g

Easy vegetable curry

SERVES 4

2 tablespoons (30 ml) olive oil
1 aubergine, quartered then sliced
1 red pepper, deseeded and sliced
1 yellow pepper, deseeded and sliced
150 g cauliflower florets
100 g button mushrooms, halved
1 courgette, halved and sliced
500 g jar curry sauce

1 Heat the oil in a large frying pan or wok, and stir-fry the aubergine and peppers together for 4 minutes or until golden.
2 Add the cauliflower, mushrooms and courgette, then stir-fry for a few more minutes.
3 Stir in the curry sauce and half a jar of water. Bring to the boil.
4 Simmer for 6–8 minutes or until the cauliflower is tender. Serve with cooked wholegrain rice.

Nutritional analysis (per serving)

Calories	160 kcal
Protein	4.5 g
Carbohydrate	13 g
Total sugars*	9.8 g
Fat	10 g
Saturates	1.0 g
Fibre	3.2 g
Salt**	1.8 g

Vegetable risotto with cashew nuts

SERVES 4

2 tablespoons (30 ml) olive oil
1 small onion, chopped
1 small red pepper, chopped
1 bay leaf
1 garlic clove, crushed
300 g Arborio (risotto) rice
1 litre hot vegetable stock
85 g green beans, cut into 2 cm lengths
125 g frozen peas
2 tomatoes, deseeded and chopped
Handful of baby spinach leaves
Freshly ground black pepper
60 g cashew nuts, lightly toasted

1. Heat the olive oil in a large heavy-based pan, and cook the onion with the red pepper, bay leaf and garlic over a moderate heat, stirring frequently.
2. Stir in the rice and cook for 1–2 minutes, stirring constantly until the grains are coated with oil and translucent.
3. Add half the hot vegetable stock and bring to the boil. Reduce the heat and simmer gently until the liquid is absorbed. Add the remaining stock, a ladleful at a time, stirring and continue to simmer until the rice is almost tender. Add the green beans, peas and tomatoes, and continue cooking for a further 5 minutes. (The total cooking time should be around 25 minutes. Perfect risotto should be thick and creamy, and the rice should still have a little bite.)
4. Add the spinach leaves and stir until the leaves have wilted. Remove from the heat.
5. Season to taste with the freshly ground black pepper then scatter over the cashew nuts. Serve on warmed plates.

Nutritional analysis (per serving)

Calories	450 kcal
Protein	10 g
Carbohydrate	72 g
Total sugars*	7.0 g
Fat	15 g
Saturates	2.8 g
Fibre	4.7 g
Salt**	0.1 g

* includes sugars found naturally in foods
** excludes salt added to the recipe

Bean and pasta salad with pumpkin seeds and feta

SERVES 4

200 g wholewheat pasta shapes
85 g pumpkin seeds
400 g tin red kidney beans in water, rinsed and drained
150 g baby plum tomatoes, halved
1 yellow pepper, deseeded and chopped
1 bunch salad onions, trimmed and finely sliced
200 g pack feta cheese, crumbled
40 g flat-leaf parsley, chopped
1 lemon, zest and juice of
2 tablespoons (30 ml) olive oil
Low-sodium salt and freshly ground black pepper

1. Preheat the oven to 220°C (gas mark 7). Cook the pasta shapes according to packet instructions. Drain.
2. Place the pumpkin seeds on a baking tray lined with baking parchment and place in the oven for 8–10 minutes, turning once, until light brown.
3. Place the beans in a large serving bowl with the pasta.
4. Add the tomatoes, peppers, onions, feta, parsley and toasted pumpkin seeds.
5. Use a fork to whisk together the lemon juice, zest, olive oil and seasoning. Drizzle over the salad and mix well to combine.

Nutritional analysis (per serving)

Calories	563 kcal
Protein	26 g
Carbohydrate	58 g
Total sugars*	6.0 g
Fat	27 g
Saturates	9.4 g
Fibre	11 g
Salt**	1.8 g

Tofu and vegetable stir-fry

SERVES 4

2 tablespoons (30 ml) light soy sauce
2 tablespoons (30 ml) rice wine vinegar
1 tablespoon (15 ml) caster sugar
1 fresh red chilli, deseeded and finely chopped
2 teaspoons (10 ml) Chinese five-spice powder
350 g tofu, cut into chunks
250 g rice
1 tablespoon (15 ml) groundnut oil
2 red and 1 yellow medium peppers, deseeded and sliced
200 g broccoli, cut into florets
1 heaped teaspoon cornflour
4 tablespoons (60 ml) cold water
2 teaspoons (10 ml) toasted sesame seeds

1. Mix the soy sauce, vinegar, sugar, chilli and five-spice powder in a shallow dish, then add the tofu and coat well. Cover and marinate for 1–2 hours if possible. When ready to cook, drain the tofu, reserving the marinade.
2. Cook the rice according to the pack instructions.
3. Heat half the oil in a wok over a high heat. Add the tofu (you might need to do this in batches). Stir-fry for 1–2 minutes, until golden, then remove to a warm plate.
4. Add the remaining oil to the pan, then stir-fry the peppers and broccoli for 3 minutes or until just tender.
5. Stir the cornflour and water into the reserved marinade and add to the pan, along with the tofu. Cook briefly until thickened. Add a little hot water if needed, to give a rich sauce. Serve with the rice, scattered with the sesame seeds.

Nutritional analysis (per serving)

Calories	405 kcal
Protein	16 g
Carbohydrate	65 g
Total sugars*	9.8 g
Fat	11 g
Saturates	1.7 g
Fibre	3.0 g
Salt**	0.1 g

Lentil and vegetable dhal with cashew nuts

SERVES 4

2 tablespoons (30 ml) sunflower oil
2 onions, chopped
2 garlic cloves, crushed
1 teaspoon (5 ml) ground cumin
2 teaspoons (10 ml) ground coriander
1 teaspoon (5 ml) turmeric
175 g red lentils
750 ml vegetable stock
2 carrots, diced
85 g courgettes, sliced
125 g frozen peas
125 g cashew nuts, toasted
1 tablespoon (15 ml) lemon juice
A little low-sodium salt
A small handful of fresh coriander, finely chopped

1. Heat the oil in a heavy-based pan and sauté the onions for 5 minutes. Add the garlic and spices, and continue cooking for one minute while stirring continuously.
2. Add the lentils, stock, carrots and courgettes. Bring to the boil. Cover and simmer for about 20 minutes, adding the peas 5 minutes before the end of the cooking time.
3. Stir in the cashew nuts then season with the lemon juice and low-sodium salt. Finally, stir in the fresh coriander.

Nutritional analysis (per serving)

Calories	434 kcal
Protein	19 g
Carbohydrate	43 g
Total sugars*	11 g
Fat	22 g
Saturates	3.8 g
Fibre	7.0 g
Salt**	0.1 g

Pasta with broccoli and pine nuts

SERVES 4

300 g wholewheat pasta shapes
2 tablespoons (30 ml) olive oil
400 g broccoli, cut into small florets
1 garlic clove, thinly sliced
2 tablespoons (30 ml) pine nuts
1 lemon, juice of
25 g fresh basil
6 tablespoons freshly grated Parmesan

1. Cook the pasta in a large pan of boiling water for 10 minutes, according to the pack instructions.
2. Halfway through the pasta's cooking time, heat 1 tablespoon of the oil in a wok or large frying pan. Stir-fry the broccoli for 3 minutes, then add the garlic and cook for 2 minutes. Season.
3. Drain the pasta and return to the pan. Stir in the remaining oil, broccoli, pine nuts, lemon juice, basil leaves and grated cheese. Serve immediately.

Nutritional analysis (per serving)

Calories	457 kcal
Protein	20 g
Carbohydrate	59 g
Total sugars*	3.6 g
Fat	17 g
Saturates	4.4 g
Fibre	9.0 g
Salt**	0.3 g

Roast ratatouille

SERVES 4

3 medium courgettes, sliced
1 large red onion, peeled, halved and cut into thin wedges
1 red and 1 yellow pepper, deseeded and cut into chunks
1 medium aubergine, halved lengthways and sliced
3–4 garlic cloves, roughly chopped
1 teaspoon olive oil
6–8 ripe tomatoes, cut into large chunks
1 tablespoon extra virgin olive oil
Salt and freshly ground black pepper

1. Preheat the oven to 220°C (gas mark 7).
2. Put the courgettes, onion, peppers, aubergine and garlic into a non-stick roasting pan, large enough to fit them in one and a half layers. Toss with 1 teaspoon olive oil.
3. Roast for 20 minutes, stirring two or three times. Remove from the oven, stir in the tomatoes, and cook for 10 minutes more, until the tomatoes are soft and all the vegetables cooked. Remove from the oven, stir in the extra virgin olive oil, season to taste, and serve.
4. Stir in fresh basil and toss with pasta for a simple supper.

Nutritional analysis (per serving)

Calories	170 kcal
Protein	4.3 g
Carbohydrate	18 g
Total sugars*	16 g
Fat	9.6 g
Saturates	1.5 g
Fibre	5.2 g
Salt**	0.1 g

* includes sugars found naturally in foods
** excludes salt added to the recipe

Roasted Mediterranean vegetables with pine nuts

SERVES 4

1 aubergine
3 courgettes
2 red peppers
1 red onion
2 garlic cloves, crushed
A few sprigs of rosemary
3 tablespoons (45 ml) extra virgin olive oil
About 12 black olives
1–2 tablespoons (15–30 ml) pine nuts, toasted

1 Preheat the oven to 200°C (gas mark 6).
2 Trim, then slice the aubergine and courgettes into wide strips. Remove the seeds from the peppers and cut them into wide strips. Cut the red onion into wedges.
3 Place the vegetables in a large roasting tin with the garlic and rosemary. Drizzle over the olive oil and toss lightly so that the vegetables are well coated in the oil.
4 Roast in the oven for about 30 minutes until the vegetables are slightly charred on the outside and tender in the middle. Mix with the black olives. Scatter over the toasted pine nuts.

Nutritional analysis (per serving)

Calories	176 kcal
Protein	3.8 g
Carbohydrate	12 g
Total sugars*	10 g
Fat	13 g
Saturates	1.7 g
Fibre	3.9 g
Salt**	0.5 g

Puy lentil and tomato salad with walnuts

SERVES 4

250 g cooked puy lentils
1 red onion, finely chopped
225 g cherry tomatoes, halved
2 tablespoons (30 ml) chopped fresh parsley or mint
3 tablespoons (45 ml) extra virgin olive oil
1 tablespoon (15 ml) red wine vinegar
Salt and freshly ground black pepper
60 g walnut pieces
125 g pack ready-washed salad leaves

1 Put the lentils in a bowl, and mix with the red onion, tomatoes and chopped herbs.
2 Place the olive oil and red wine vinegar in a bottle or screw-top glass jar and shake together. Pour the dressing over the lentil salad.
3 Toss lightly and season with salt and pepper.
4 Arrange the salad leaves on a serving plate, pile the lentil salad on top then sprinkle with the walnuts.

Nutritional analysis (per serving)

Calories	266 kcal
Protein	8.6 g
Carbohydrate	16 g
Total sugars*	4.5 g
Fat	19 g
Saturates	2.1 g
Fibre	4.0 g
Salt**	0.1 g

Vegetable chilli with beans

SERVES 4

2 tablespoons (30 ml) sunflower oil
1 onion, chopped
2 red peppers, deseeded and cut into chunks
1 tablespoon mild chilli powder
1 large carrot, peeled and cut into chunks
2 sweet potatoes, peeled and cut into chunks
400 g can chopped tomatoes
200 ml hot vegetable stock
1 courgette, sliced
410 g can red kidney beans, drained
50 g green beans, trimmed and halved

1. Heat the oil in a large pan. Add the onion and cook over a medium heat for 5 minutes until softened, then add the peppers and cook for 2 minutes.
2. Add the chilli powder and stir for 1 minute.
3. Stir in the carrot and sweet potatoes, then add the tomatoes and stock, and simmer for 15–20 minutes.
4. Add the courgette and kidney beans, and simmer for a further 5 minutes. Finally, add the green beans and simmer for 5–10 minutes, or until all the vegetables are tender. Serve with basmati rice.

Nutritional analysis (per serving)

Calories	267 kcal
Protein	10 g
Carbohydrate	44 g
Total sugars*	18 g
Fat	6.9 g
Saturates	1.0 g
Fibre	11 g
Salt**	0.2 g

* includes sugars found naturally in foods
** excludes salt added to the recipe

Rice with chickpeas and spinach

SERVES 4

225 g basmati rice
1 lemon, zest of
425 g can chickpeas, drained
125 g baby spinach leaves
60 g black olives, pitted
A little low-sodium salt and freshly ground black pepper

1. Put the basmati rice, lemon zest and 400 ml water in a large saucepan. Bring to the boil. Cover, reduce the heat and simmer for 15 minutes.
2. Add the chickpeas and continue cooking over a gentle heat for a further 5–10 minutes until the liquid has been absorbed and the rice is cooked.
3. Add the spinach and let stand for another couple of minutes. Stir in the olives, season with the low-sodium salt and pepper, and serve.

Nutritional analysis (per serving)

Calories	316 kcal
Protein	11 g
Carbohydrate	59 g
Total sugars*	1.2 g
Fat	3.8 g
Saturates	0.4 g
Fibre	4.3 g
Salt**	1.0 g

SOUP

Butternut squash soup

SERVES 4

1 medium butternut squash
1 litre vegetable stock
1 large onion, chopped
1 small swede, peeled and chopped
2 tablespoons (30 ml) extra virgin olive oil
A little low-sodium salt and freshly ground black pepper

1. Peel the butternut squash and cut the flesh into chunks.
2. Place the vegetable stock, butternut squash, onion and swede in a large saucepan. Bring to the boil, lower the heat, cover and simmer for about 20 minutes until the vegetables are tender.
3. Remove from the heat and liquidise with the olive oil until smooth, using a blender, food processor or hand blender.
4. Return to the saucepan to heat through. Season the soup with the low-sodium salt and freshly ground black pepper.

Nutritional analysis (per serving)

Calories	76 kcal
Protein	0.8 g
Carbohydrate	6.2 g
Total sugars*	3.4 g
Fat	5.6 g
Saturates	0.8 g
Fibre	1.2 g
Salt**	0.1 g

* includes sugars found naturally in foods
** excludes salt added to the recipe

Mediterranean vegetable soup

SERVES 4

2 tablespoons (30 ml) extra virgin olive oil
1 onion, thinly sliced
2 garlic cloves, finely chopped
1 red and 1 green pepper, deseeded and sliced
2 courgettes, trimmed and sliced
450 g tomatoes, skinned and quartered, or 400 g tinned tomatoes
Half an aubergine, diced
1 litre vegetable stock or water
A little low-sodium salt, to taste
1 tablespoon (15 ml) pesto

1. Heat the olive oil in a large saucepan. Add the onion and garlic, and sauté over a moderate heat for about 5 minutes until translucent.
2. Add the prepared vegetables and tomatoes, and stock or water, and then bring to the boil. Simmer for about 25–30 minutes or until the vegetables are tender.
3. Allow the soup to cool slightly for a couple of minutes, then liquidise using a hand blender or conventional blender. Season to taste with the low-sodium salt.
4. Serve in individual bowls, adding a teaspoon of pesto to each bowl immediately before serving.

Nutritional analysis (per serving)

Calories	162 kcal
Protein	4.4 g
Carbohydrate	16 g
Total sugars*	13 g
Fat	9.6 g
Saturates	1.9 g
Fibre	4.1 g
Salt**	0.1 g

Pumpkin soup

SERVES 4

2 tablespoons (30 ml) extra virgin olive oil
1 onion, chopped
2.5 cm piece fresh ginger, peeled and grated
1 garlic clove, crushed
½ teaspoon (2.5 ml) grated nutmeg
½ teaspoon (2.5 ml) ground coriander
1 carrot, sliced
1 medium potato, peeled and chopped
700 g pumpkin flesh, chopped
600 ml vegetable stock
A little low-sodium salt and freshly ground black pepper

1. Heat the olive oil in a large saucepan, add the onion and sauté over moderate heat for about 5 minutes, until translucent. Add the ginger, garlic, nutmeg and coriander, and cook for a further minute.
2. Add the prepared vegetables, stir well, cover and continue cooking gently for a further 5 minutes. Add the stock, bring to the boil, reduce the heat and simmer for about 20 minutes or until the vegetables are tender.
3. Liquidise the soup using a hand blender or conventional blender. Add a little more water or stock if you want a thinner consistency. Season to taste with the low-sodium salt and black pepper.

Nutritional analysis (per serving)

Calories	121 kcal
Protein	2.6 g
Carbohydrate	15 g
Total sugars*	6.8 g
Fat	6.0 g
Saturates	1.0 g
Fibre	3.2 g
Salt**	0.1 g

Lentil soup

SERVES 4

2 tablespoons olive oil
1 onion, sliced
2 leeks, sliced
2 carrots, sliced
2 stalks celery, thinly sliced
2 potatoes, diced
175 g red lentils
1.5 litres vegetable stock
½ lemon, juice of
2 tablespoons chopped fresh flat-leaf parsley
A little low-sodium salt and freshly ground black pepper

1. Heat the olive oil in a large heavy-based saucepan. Add the onion, leeks, carrots, celery and potato, and cook gently for about 10 minutes or until the vegetables have softened, but not coloured.
2. Add the lentils. Pour in the stock and bring to the boil. Simmer, partially covered, for a further 15–20 minutes until the vegetables and lentils are tender.
3. Add the lemon juice, season to taste with a little salt and black pepper, and stir in the fresh herbs.

Nutritional analysis (per serving)

Calories	245 kcal
Protein	12 g
Carbohydrate	37 g
Total sugars*	4.0 g
Fat	6.4 g
Saturates	<1 g
Fibre	3.9 g
Salt**	0.1 g

Vegetable soup

SERVES 4

2 tablespoons (30 ml) extra virgin olive oil
1 onion, finely sliced
450 g (approx 6) carrots, sliced
225 g (approx 2) parsnips, diced
1 litre vegetable stock
1 bay leaf
125 g green beans, topped, tailed and halved
125 g frozen peas
A small handful basil leaves, roughly torn
A little low-sodium salt and freshly ground black pepper

1. Heat the olive oil in a heavy-based saucepan over a moderate heat. Add the onion and cook gently for about 5 minutes until softened.
2. Add the carrots and parsnips to the pan, and continue to cook over a moderate heat for 5 minutes, stirring occasionally, until the vegetables soften a little.
3. Add the stock and bay leaf, and bring to the boil. Simmer for 10 minutes, add the beans and peas and cook for a further 5 minutes.
4. Remove and discard the bay leaf. Liquidise the soup using a hand blender or conventional blender. Stir in the basil and season with low-sodium salt and freshly ground pepper.

Nutritional analysis (per serving)

Calories	124 kcal
Protein	3.5 g
Carbohydrate	13 g
Total sugars*	7.3 g
Fat	6.6 g
Saturates	1.0 g
Fibre	5.5 g
Salt**	0.1 g

* includes sugars found naturally in foods
** excludes salt added to the recipe

Chicken soup

SERVES 4

2 tablespoons olive oil
2 onions, finely sliced
2 potatoes, peeled and diced
2 stalks celery, thinly sliced
1 carrot, thinly sliced
2 skinless chicken breasts, diced
1 litre chicken stock
400 g tin chickpeas, drained and rinsed
1 bay leaf
1 tablespoon chopped chives or parsley

1. Heat the olive oil in a large, heavy-based saucepan. Add the onion, potato, celery, carrot and diced chicken. Cook gently for about 5 minutes or until the vegetables have softened.
2. Pour in the stock, add the chickpeas and bay leaf, and bring to the boil. Simmer, partially covered, for a further 15–20 minutes until the vegetables are tender.
3. Stir in the fresh herbs and serve.

Nutritional analysis (per serving)

Calories	303 kcal
Protein	27 g
Carbohydrate	28 g
Total sugars*	6.3 g
Fat	10 g
Saturates	1.6 g
Fibre	5.3 g
Salt**	0.5 g

Carrot soup with fresh coriander

SERVES 4

2 tablespoons (30 ml) extra virgin olive oil
1 onion, finely sliced
1 garlic clove, crushed
4–6 carrots, sliced
1 litre vegetable stock
1 bay leaf
A little low-sodium salt and freshly ground black pepper
A handful of fresh coriander, roughly chopped

1. Heat the olive oil in a heavy-based saucepan over a moderate heat. Add the onion and sauté gently for about 5 minutes until it is translucent.
2. Add the garlic and cook for a further 1–2 minutes. Add the carrots, stock and bay leaf to the pan, stir, then bring to the boil. Simmer for 15 minutes or until the vegetables are tender.
3. Allow the soup to cool slightly for a couple of minutes. Remove and discard the bay leaf. Liquidise the soup using a hand blender or conventional blender. Season to taste with low-sodium salt and pepper, then stir in the fresh coriander.

Nutritional analysis (per serving)

Calories	98 kcal
Protein	1.0 g
Carbohydrate	11 g
Total sugars*	9.6 g
Fat	5.9 g
Saturates	<1 g
Fibre	3.0 g
Salt**	0.1 g

Tomato and chickpea soup

Serves 4

500 ml vegetable stock
1 small red onion, chopped
1–2 garlic cloves, crushed
400 g tinned chopped tomatoes
200 g tinned chickpeas
1 small courgette, trimmed and finely sliced
60 g fine green beans
60 g small wholewheat pasta shapes
Small handful basil leaves, torn
1 tablespoon (15 ml) olive oil

1. Pour the vegetable stock into a large saucepan. Bring to the boil and add the onion, garlic, tomatoes, chickpeas, courgette and green beans. Lower the heat, cover and simmer for 10 minutes until the vegetables are tender.
2. Add the pasta and continue cooking for a further 3–5 minutes or according to the cooking times on the packet. Stir in the torn basil leaves.
3. Serve the soup hot in individual bowls. Drizzle with the oil.

Nutritional analysis (per serving)

Calories	328 kcal
Protein	15 g
Carbohydrate	49 g
Total sugars*	9.9 g
Fat	9.5 g
Saturates	1.3 g
Fibre	9.5 g
Salt**	0.8 g

SAVOURY SNACKS

Pitta crisps

MAKES ABOUT 24

2 pitta breads (wholemeal or white)
A little olive oil

1 Preheat the oven to 200°C (gas mark 6).
2 Split the pitta breads through the middle and open out so that you have four pieces.
3 Cut each piece into triangles. Arrange on a baking tray, brush with a little oil, and bake in the oven for 5–7 minutes until they become crisp and golden.

Nutritional analysis (each)

Calories	25 kcal
Protein	0.6 g
Carbohydrate	3.6 g
Total sugars*	0.2 g
Fat	1.0 g
Saturates	0.1 g
Fibre	0.3 g
Salt**	0.1 g

Hummus with pine nuts

SERVES 4

400 g tinned chickpeas (in water)
1 garlic clove, crushed
2 tablespoons (30 ml) extra virgin olive oil
1 tablespoon (15 ml) tahini (sesame seed paste)
½ lemon, juice of
2–4 tablespoons (30–60 ml) water
A little low-sodium salt and freshly ground black pepper
1–2 tablespoons (15–30 ml) pine nuts

1 Drain and rinse the chickpeas. Reserve 1–2 tablespoons of chickpeas. Put the remainder in a food processor or blender with the garlic, olive oil, tahini, lemon juice and water. Whizz until smooth, add a little low-sodium salt and freshly ground black pepper, and process again.
2 Taste to check the seasoning. Add extra water if necessary to give the desired consistency.
3 Meanwhile lightly toast the pine nuts under a hot grill for 3–4 minutes until they are lightly coloured but not brown (watch carefully as they colour quickly).
4 Stir in the reserved whole chickpeas. Spoon into a shallow dish. Scatter over the pine nuts and drizzle over a few drops of olive oil. Chill in the fridge for at least 2 hours before serving. Serve with olives, cherry tomatoes, carrot, cucumber and pepper strips, or spread on rye crackers or rice cakes for a delicious, nourishing lunch.

Nutritional analysis (per serving)

Calories	224 kcal
Protein	8.6 g
Carbohydrate	14 g
Total sugars*	1.0 g
Fat	15 g
Saturates	1.9 g
Fibre	4.1 g
Salt**	0.1 g

Guacamole

SERVES 4

2 ripe avocados
2 tablespoons (30 ml) lemon or lime juice
½ small red onion, finely chopped
1 clove of garlic, crushed
2 medium tomatoes, skinned and chopped
2 tablespoons (30 ml) fresh coriander, finely chopped
Sea salt and freshly ground black pepper
Cayenne pepper and extra virgin olive oil

1. Halve the avocados and scoop out the flesh. Mash the avocado flesh with the lemon or lime juice.
2. Add the remaining ingredients (except the cayenne pepper and extra virgin olive oil), mixing well. Alternatively, you can process the ingredients in a food processor to a coarse purée.
3. Check the seasoning, adding a little more black pepper or lemon juice if necessary. Chill.
4. Just before serving, sprinkle with a little cayenne pepper and drizzle with olive oil.

Nutritional analysis (per serving)

Calories	168 kcal
Protein	2.0 g
Carbohydrate	4.8 g
Total sugars*	3.1 g
Fat	16 g
Saturates	3.2 g
Fibre	3.2 g
Salt**	0.1 g

Tomato salsa

SERVES 4

2 large ripe tomatoes or 4 ripe plum tomatoes, skinned, deseeded and finely diced
1–2 tablespoons (15–30 ml) chopped fresh parsley or coriander
1 teaspoon (5 ml) finely chopped fresh chilli (or according to your taste)
1 small clove of garlic, crushed
1 tablespoon (15 ml) olive oil
2 spring onions, finely chopped
2 tablespoons (30 ml) lemon or lime juice

1. Combine all the ingredients in a bowl.
2. Chill in the fridge for at least 2 hours before serving. Serve with crudités, and grilled or roasted vegetables.

Nutritional analysis (per serving)

Calories	64 kcal
Protein	0.6 g
Carbohydrate	2.6 g
Total sugars*	2.6 g
Fat	5.7 g
Saturates	0.9 g
Fibre	0.8 g
Salt**	0.1 g

* includes sugars found naturally in foods
** excludes salt added to the recipe

Aubergine dip

SERVES 4
1 aubergine
2 tablespoons (30 ml) lemon juice
2 tablespoons (30 ml) olive oil
2 tablespoons (30 ml) chopped parsley
1 tablespoon (15 ml) tahini
1 clove of garlic, crushed
Freshly ground black pepper

1 Preheat the oven to 200°C (gas mark 6). Prick the aubergine all over with a fork, place on a baking tray and bake for about 40 minutes until soft.
2 Allow to cool then purée in a blender or food processor with the remaining ingredients. Chill.

Nutritional analysis (per serving)

Calories	113 kcal
Protein	2.1 g
Carbohydrate	1.0 g
Total sugars*	0.8 g
Fat	11 g
Saturates	1.6 g
Fibre	1.7 g
Salt**	0.1 g

SWEET SNACKS

Banana cake

MAKES 12 SLICES

2 large ripe bananas
250 ml orange juice
300 g self-raising flour (half wholemeal, half white)
125 g brown sugar
Salt, pinch
½ teaspoon each of mixed spice and cinnamon
1 egg
1 tablespoon (15 ml) oil

1. Mash the bananas with the orange juice.
2. Mix together the flour, sugar, salt and spices in a bowl.
3. Add the banana juice mixture together with the egg and oil. Combine.
4. Spoon into a lightly oiled 900 g loaf tin.
5. Bake at 170°C (gas mark 3) for about an hour. Check the cake is done by inserting a skewer or knife into the centre. It should come out clean.

Nutritional analysis (per serving)

Calories	167 kcal
Protein	3.2 g
Carbohydrate	37 g
Total sugars*	18 g
Fat	1.9 g
Saturates	0.4 g
Fibre	1.1 g
Salt**	0.3 g

Fruit cake

MAKES 10 SLICES

225 g stoned dates, roughly chopped
300 ml water
85 g wholemeal flour
85 g plain flour
3 teaspoons (15 ml) baking powder
1 teaspoon (5 ml) ground mixed spice
500 g dried, mixed fruit
60 g ground almonds
85 ml orange juice

1. Preheat the oven to 170°C (gas mark 3), and line a 900 g loaf tin with baking parchment.
2. Put the dates and water in a pan and bring to the boil. Remove the pan from the heat and set aside.
3. Put the two flours, baking powder and mixed spice into a bowl. Add the mixed fruit and ground almonds, and stir to combine.
4. Stir in the date mixture and the orange juice. Mix well. Spoon into the loaf tin.
5. Bake for 45–50 minutes, or until a skewer inserted comes out clean.
6. Turn out on to a wire rack and cool.

Nutritional analysis (per serving)

Calories	294 kcal
Protein	5.0 g
Carbohydrate	65 g
Total sugars*	51 g
Fat	3.9 g
Saturates	0.3 g
Fibre	3.4 g
Salt**	0.5 g

Oaty apple crumble

SERVES 4
700 g cooking apples, peeled and sliced
85 g clear honey
½ teaspoon cinnamon
4 tablespoons water

For the topping:
125 g plain flour
85 g olive oil margarine
50 g oats
75 g brown sugar

1. Preheat the oven to 190°C (gas mark 5).
2. Place the apples, honey and cinnamon in a deep baking dish. Combine well and pour the water over.
3. For the crumble topping, put the flour in a bowl and rub in the margarine until the mixture resembles coarse bread-crumbs. Mix in the oats and sugar. Alternatively, mix in a food mixer or processor.
4. Sprinkle the crumble mixture over the fruit. Bake for 20–25 minutes until the topping is golden and fruit is tender.

Nutritional analysis (per serving)

Calories	331 kcal
Protein	3.2 g
Carbohydrate	54 g
Total sugars*	32 g
Fat	13 g
Saturates	2.5 g
Fibre	2.6 g
Salt**	0.3 g

* includes sugars found naturally in foods
** excludes salt added to the recipe

Apple muffins

MAKES 12 MUFFINS
60 ml sunflower oil
125 g soft brown sugar
2 eggs
125 ml milk
1 teaspoon (5 ml) vanilla extract
2 apples, peeled, cored and grated
225 g self-raising flour

1. Preheat the oven to 190°C (gas mark 5).
2. Combine the oil, sugar, eggs, milk and vanilla extract in a bowl.
3. Stir in the grated apples and flour.
4. Spoon the mixture into non-stick muffin tins. Bake for 15–20 minutes until golden brown.

Nutritional analysis (per serving)

Calories	172 kcal
Protein	3.4 g
Carbohydrate	27 g
Total sugars*	13 g
Fat	6.6 g
Saturates	1.1 g
Fibre	0.9 g
Salt**	0.2 g

Blueberry muffins

MAKES 12 MUFFINS
85 g margarine
2 tablespoons clear honey
1 large egg
1 teaspoon (5 ml) vanilla extract
200 ml skimmed milk
225 g white self-raising flour
125 g fresh blueberries

1 Preheat the oven to 200°C (gas mark 6).
2 Line 12 muffin tins with paper muffin cases.
3 Mix together the margarine and honey until smooth. In a separate bowl beat the egg, vanilla and milk, then add to the margarine/honey mixture together with 2 tablespoons of the flour. Beat the mixture until smooth, then fold in the remaining flour. Stir until just combined. Gently fold in the blueberries.
4 Spoon the mixture into the prepared muffin tins – about two-thirds full – and then bake for 18–20 minutes until the muffins are risen and golden.

Nutritional analysis (per serving)

Calories	147 kcal
Protein	3.0 g
Carbohydrate	20 g
Total sugars*	6.0 g
Fat	6.7 g
Saturates	1.4 g
Fibre	0.9 g
Salt**	0.3 g

Raisin muffins

MAKES 12 MUFFINS
125 g white self-raising flour
125 g wholemeal self-raising flour
1 tablespoon (15ml) oil
40 g soft brown sugar
1 egg
150 ml skimmed milk
60 g raisins

1 Preheat the oven to 220°C (gas mark 7).
2 Mix the flours together in a bowl. Add the oil, sugar, egg and milk. Mix well.
3 Stir in the dried fruit.
4 Spoon in to a non-stick muffin tray and bake for approx 15 minutes, until golden brown.

Nutritional analysis (per serving)

Calories	113 kcal
Protein	3.4 g
Carbohydrate	22 g
Total sugars*	7.9 g
Fat	1.0 g
Saturates	0.3 g
Fibre	1.4 g
Salt**	0.1 g

Walnut and date flapjacks

MAKES 12 FLAPJACKS
150 g butter or margarine
60 g light brown sugar
5 tablespoons golden syrup
200 g porridge oats
60 g chopped dates
100 g chopped walnuts

1 Preheat the oven to 180°C (gas mark 4). Lightly oil a 23 cm-square baking tin.
2 Put the butter or margarine, sugar and syrup in a heavy-based saucepan and heat together, stirring occasionally, until the butter has melted. Remove from the heat.
3 Mix in the oats, dates and walnuts until thoroughly combined.
4 Transfer the mixture into the prepared tin, level the surface and bake in the oven for 20–25 minutes until golden brown around the edges but still soft in the middle.
5 Leave in the tin to cool. While still warm, score into 12 bars with a sharp knife.

Nutritional analysis (per serving)

Calories	286 kcal
Protein	3.6 g
Carbohydrate	31 g
Total sugars*	17 g
Fat	17 g
Saturates	7.0 g
Fibre	1.6 g
Salt**	0.3 g

* includes sugars found naturally in foods
** excludes salt added to the recipe

Fruit and nut cookies

MAKES 20 COOKIES
225 g wholemeal self-raising flour
40 g brown sugar
85 g dried fruit
60 g chopped walnuts or almonds
2 tablespoons (30 ml) oil
1 egg
4–5 tablespoons skimmed milk

1 Combine the flour, sugar, fruit and nuts in a bowl.
2 Stir in the oil, egg and milk, and lightly mix together until you have a stiff dough.
3 Place spoonfuls of the mixture on to a lightly oiled baking tray.
4 Bake at 180°C (gas mark 4) for 12–15 minutes, until golden brown.

Nutritional analysis (per serving)

Calories	90 kcal
Protein	2.5 g
Carbohydrate	13 g
Total sugars*	5.5 g
Fat	3.8 g
Saturates	0.4 g
Fibre	1.2 g
Salt**	9.1 g

Baked vanilla cheesecake

SERVES 8
1 sponge flan base
225 g cottage cheese
150 g plain yoghurt
1 teaspoon (5 ml) vanilla extract
2 eggs, separated
25 g cornflour
85 g caster sugar

1. Preheat the oven to 130°C (gas mark 1).
2. Trim the flan base to fit a 22 cm loose-bottomed cake tin.
3. Mix the cottage cheese, yoghurt, vanilla extract, egg yolks and cornflour together until smooth. Alternatively, process in a food processor until well combined.
4. In a separate bowl beat the egg whites with an electric whisk until they are stiff. While whisking at a low speed, slowly add the sugar. Fold the whites into the cottage cheese mixture.
5. Spoon or pour carefully on to the sponge flan base and bake in the oven for 45 minutes or until there is no wobble in the middle. Take out of the oven and allow to cool for 15–20 minutes.
6. Chill in the fridge before serving.

Nutritional analysis (per serving)

Calories	178 kcal
Protein	8.5 g
Carbohydrate	28 g
Total sugars*	21 g
Fat	4.4 g
Saturates	1.3 g
Fibre	0.2 g
Salt**	0.3 g

Cereal bars

MAKES 12 BARS
175 g oats
85 g no added sugar muesli
150 g dried fruit mixture
3 tablespoons (45 ml) honey, clear or set
2 egg whites
175 ml apple juice

1. Preheat the oven to 180°C (gas mark 4).
2. Combine the oats, muesli and dried fruit in a bowl.
3. Warm the honey in a small saucepan until it is runny. Add to the bowl.
4. Stir in the remaining ingredients.
5. Press the mixture into a lightly oiled, 18 × 28 cm baking tin. Bake for 20–25 minutes, until golden. When cool, cut into bars.

Nutritional analysis (per serving)

Calories	147 kcal
Protein	3.3 g
Carbohydrate	31 g
Total sugars*	17 g
Fat	1.9 g
Saturates	0.1 g
Fibre	1.8 g
Salt**	0.1 g

RESOURCES

Useful websites and helplines

British Nutrition Foundation

www.nutrition.org.uk

The website of the British Nutrition Foundation, contains information, fact sheets and educational resources on nutrition and health.

Food Standards Agency

www.eatwell.gov.uk

The website of the government's Food Standards Agency has news of nutrition surveys, nutrition and health information.

American Dietetic Association

www.eatright.org

The website of the American Dietetic Association, gives nutrition news, tips and resources.

British Dietetic Association

www.bda.uk.com

The website of the British Dietetic Association includes fact sheets and information on healthy eating for children. It also provides details of Registered Dietitians working in private practice.

Gatorade Sports Science Institute

www.gssiweb.com

This website provides a good database of articles and consensus papers on nutritional topics written by experts.

Vegetarian Society

www.vegsoc.org

This website provides information on vegetarian nutrition for children as well as general nutrition, health and recipes.

Weight Loss Resources

www.weightlossresources.co.uk

This UK website provides excellent information on weight loss, fitness and healthy eating as well as a comprehensive calorie database and a personalised weight loss programme.

beat (the eating disorders association)
www.b-eat.co.uk
Adult helpline: 0845 634 1414
Youthline: 0845 634 7650
beat is a national charity, based in the UK, providing information, help and support for people affected by eating disorders and, in particular, anorexia and bulimia nervosa.

Disordered Eating
www.disordered-eating.co.uk
Provides comprehensive information about disordered eating and eating disorders.

Anorexia and Bulimia Care
www.anorexiabulimiacare.co.uk
Anorexia and Bulimia Care is a national Christian charity, providing advice and support for sufferers and their families, information for teachers and health professionals, and training for counsellors.

National Centre for Eating Disorders
www.eating-disorders.org.uk
The National Centre for Eating Disorders is an independent organisation set up to provide solutions for all eating problems and eating disorders.

Female Athlete Triad Coalition
www.femaleathletetriad.org
This website provides information for athletes, coaches and health professionals on the female athlete triad.

Further reading

Applegate, L., *Eat Smart Play Hard,* Rodale, 2001
Bean, A., *Food For Fitness* 3rd edition, A & C Black, 2007
Bean, A., *The Complete Guide to Sports Nutrition,* A & C Black, 2009
Burke, L., *Practical Sports Nutrition,* Human Kinetics 2007
Costain, L., Kellow J. & Walton R., *The Calorie, Carb and Fat Bible 2009,* Weight Loss Resources
Jeukendrup A. & Glesson M., *Sport Nutrition,* Human Kinetics 2004

Paterson, A., *Beating Eating Disorders Step by Step: A Self-help Guide for Recovery,* Jessica Kingsley Publishers, 2008

Treasure J., *Anorexia Nervosa: A Survival Guide for Families, Friends and Sufferers,* Psychology Press, 1997

INDEX

E

F

G

H

I

L

M

O

P

ALSO AVAILABLE FROM A&C BLACK

Food for Fitness

ANITA BEAN

Food for Fitness is the bible for anyone who takes their sport, health and fitness seriously. It is packed full of information on nutrition – clearly distinguishing between myth and reality – and includes ten ready-made meal plans, plus guidance on how to develop your own. It also contains over 50 recipes for snacks, meals and drinks.

Healthy Eating for Kids

ANITA BEAN

Packed with essential up-to-date advice on healthy eating, feeding fussy eaters, dealing with an overweight child, and plenty of tips for no-hassle meals, quick snacks and lunch boxes, including brand new colour photographs of the recipes. Tested by parents and tasted by children, Anita's recipes will give you new idea and inspiration on what to feed your kids.

ALSO AVAILABLE FROM A&C BLACK

Shape Up!
CAROLINE SANDRY
Shape Up! Tailor-made Training for Female Body Shapes provides guidance to getting the best from your body shape: identifying body type and shape, setting realistic goals and developing a suitable fitness programme.

Shape Up!
JOHN SHEPHERD
Shape Up! explains the concept of body shape, helping you to identify your body type and shape, set realistic goals, develop a programme suited to your body shape and work out what is best to eat for your body type.